COMPLETE BRITISH CLOCKS

Books by Brian Loomes include

THE WHITE DIAL CLOCK
WESTMORLAND CLOCKS AND CLOCKMAKERS
LANCASHIRE CLOCKS AND CLOCKMAKERS
COUNTRY CLOCKS AND THEIR LONDON ORIGINS

COMPLETE
BRITISH CLOCKS

Brian Loomes

DAVID & CHARLES
Newton Abbot   London   North Pomfret (Vt)

Previous page. Unquestionably original oak case, made in 1741 to house the musical thirty-hour clock by Thomas Lister senior. An engraved brass plaque on the hood gives the musical notation of the melody and the owners, 'Isaac Mary Houldroyd 1741'. This very special clock was probably made for their wedding, as Isaac is believed to have been Thomas Lister's brother-in-law.

British Library Cataloguing in Publication Data

Loomes, Brian
    Complete British clocks.
    1. Clocks and watches, British – History
    I. Title
    681'.113'0941   NK7495.G7

    ISBN 0-7153-7567-9

Library of Congress Catalog Card Number: 78-66804

Typeset by Quad Typesetters Limited
Printed in Great Britain
by Butler & Tanner Limited, Frome, Somerset
for David & Charles (Publishers) Limited
Brunel House   Newton Abbot   Devon

Published in the United States of America
by David & Charles Inc
North Pomfret   Vermont 05053   USA

Contents

Preface

There is a need, it seems to me, for a work which is general enough to cover all the varying types of British clock and thereby to provide under one cover a comprehensive and up-to-date guide for the beginner in a non-technical language that he can understand. At the same time, for a book to be worthwhile, it must examine its subjects in sufficient depth for the reader to be able really to grasp an understanding of them. This book attempts to do just that. It deals with all types of clocks made in Britain before 1870. It does not cover the many types of imported clocks, most of which date from after 1840, even though many of them bear the name of a British retailer on their dials.

The connoisseur, collector, dealer, librarian, museum curator and clock enthusiast—who may already have an essential understanding of the subject, whether he has limited or extensive experience—all these, it is hoped, will find much in this book that they have not read before: new research, new opinions, new insights and new illustrations.

Important emphasis is here placed on clocks made in the provinces for, while these form the majority of those one meets with, their merits are only just beginning to be appreciated. This is especially so with the rare and interesting work of the early clocksmiths, which is examined here in some detail. Clock casework often has to be dealt with cursorily in books as the variety of styles is large and the space is short. Here I have taken a close look at some features of casework in an attempt to show differences of period, region, style and quality.

As a clock dealer I am obliged to buy every 'new' book on the subject, and find nothing more tedious and infuriating than to have to read in some of them the rehashed repetitions of the errors of horological writers of half a century ago. From this at least I will have spared the reader of this book.

Brian Loomes,
Nidderdale, 1978.

1 The Cream of Crafts

I give to William, my sonne, my Guilded watch, which cost three pounds twelve shillings: which I commonly carrie about me: it was made the same yeare that William was borne, 1589, which year is graven by the name of of the maker on the watch.

(From a will written in 1590.)

The European background—Royal Clockmakers—the London luxury market—cream of crafts—the apprenticeship system—basic clock terminology—the balance wheel—springs and weights—the fusee—David Ramsay and the French connection—the 1622 petition—the Grinkin clan—French domination continues—the British clock emerges

Domestic clockmaking in Britain began about the year 1600. For the previous half century virtually all the clocks sold in this country—and there were not all that many of them—were imported from Europe, even though some of them bear the names of native clockmakers. Some were made completely in Germany, France or the Low Countries and carried to London for sale there; others were manufactured in London by Europeans who were in temporary residence here, by men who came to stay for perhaps two or three years rather than merely for a short selling trip. Experts may argue about which circumstances applied to each of the few rare clocks that survive from that period. It does not really matter, except in academic circles: the main point is that the London market for clocks, small though it was, was monopolised by Europeans with skills that were possessed only by Europeans. There was no native British clock craft in household clocks (although there *was* a church clock trade, which was something very different).

9

Before the start of the seventeenth century, then, we are talking of barely half a dozen known makers who might claim to have a bearing on native British work, and this largely because they held the prestige appointment of Royal Clockmaker. Nicholas Urseau (or Ourseau), supposedly a Frenchman, was clockmaker to Queen Elizabeth until his death in 1590. Bartholomew Newsam, said by some to be English—though without any apparent evidence—succeeded Urseau in 1590, but remained barely a year in office. He died in 1593. Randolph Bull, also thought to have been French, took over in 1591 but was dismissed the office in 1613. These royal office-holders and the few other clockmakers in that same small clique (such as the Vallins, John and Nicholas) catered exclusively for royalty and nobility. Their works were costly in the materials used and also in the time and rare skills lavished on them. They held a monopoly trade in a cushioned luxury market.

So there was always this small and exclusive clique of Royal jewellers, men who provided costly toys for kings. One gets the impression that some of them obtained their preferment more because of their talents as courtiers and political hangers-on than because of their excellence at the craft. However they obtained their appointments, these Royal office-holders were the envied cream of the craft. They were the most powerful men not only in their own trade but in the whole of the craft society because of the unique prestige position of the clock- and watchmakers.

If you were a king or a nobleman in the early seventeenth century, the most costly thing that you could buy for yourself or your wife or mistress to show off your wealth, taste and general excellence—given that you already had a sufficiency of houses and clothing—was a watch, or a clock, or both, or dozens of them. They could tell you the time and so you had an excuse to look at them frequently. Of course, such men would have been the last people in the land to whom the time of day really mattered, because everything would revolve around them and in no way need they observe any timetable, no matter how accurately they might be able to do so.

Clocks could show you the position of the stars in the sky or the favourable conjunctions of planets from which your fortunes might be told—more dignified than reading the tea-leaves; planetary dispositions in those times were much more relevant to astrology than to astronomy, except for a very tiny band of scientists. They could play you a merry tune or a carillon of bells, thereby drawing the frequent attention of all present to admire your good sense at having caused such wonders to be constructed. They could even have automated figures—little people, birds or animals, who would come to life as if by magic and perform their amusing antics for the delight of your guests. And of course all this, bells, time-telling, star-reading, music and moving figures, could take place in or upon the most dazzling jewelled casket you could desire—thus displaying to the observing world in your own salon your wealth as well as your good taste and wisdom. Such things were the bejewelled toys of the very wealthy. They owned them for the fun they provided and for the *gloire* they reflected.

There is a story—I do not believe it, but it is interesting just the same—that Charles II, when Prince of Wales, used to take Edward East, the Royal Watchmaker, to watch his courtiers play tennis, and that to reward skilful play he would give the lucky contestant one of East's watches. It is one of the silliest stories of clock lore, and clearly untrue as the young Prince of Wales left England at the age of sixteen in 1646, fourteen years before East was made Royal Clockmaker, but it is interesting just the same because it confirms the point I am making. If Charles *did* give such rewards, was he doing it to further science, the arts, or tennis? Well, none of them of course, but because a watch was *fun* to have, a prestige item!

Most trades and crafts began at the bottom of the scale, while sophisticated exponents catered for the wealthy. That is, the mass market came first, and out of it developed the top-class luxury end of the trade: furniture, weapons, clothing, and so on. With clock- and watchmaking the exact opposite was true. It began as an exclusive trade for the very wealthiest in the land. In 1600 there was absolutely no question of the ordinary person owning a clock or watch.

At the start of the seventeenth century, then, if you were unfortunate enough to have to put your son out to a trade, the trade where the highest financial rewards lay, with the most prestige in the most noble circles, was undoubtedly clock- and watchmaking, a trade that was likely to have a booming luxury market with never a shortage of wealthy patrons whether times were bad or good. There was one problem, and that was that this luxury trade flourished only at the centre of the luxury market—London. Whether you lived in a country village, or a flourishing city such as Norwich, York or Bristol, that was not enough; it had to be London—where, in any case, it was well known that the streets were paved with gold. (Of course there *were* clockmakers in the provinces. These were the blacksmiths/clockmakers/bellfounders/locksmiths group of heavy-metal tradesmen, who made principally church and tower clocks and who had been at work in the land for over a century.)

If you were able to make the right social contacts, pull a few strings, knew the right people and could pay the fee for the prescribed seven-year apprenticeship, you could buy your son an entry into this very exclusive training academy, and at the age of thirteen or fourteen you sent him off to the big city. It was the very best chance in life that he could have.

It must have seemed like a life sentence to a young lad, being dragged out of his home by the forelock, bound, for all eternity it must have seemed, to some man he had barely set eyes on, some forbidding character who parleyed with Royalty about his goods and in whose home you were to live, perhaps with rats in the garret. Even the boldest boy must have been terrified at the prospect, and what must have hurt even more was that everyone told you how lucky you were to get the chance!

Two thousand youngsters were bound out in this way to the London masters before the century was out. Only one in four made the grade; the rest was wastage. Insanitary conditions, plague, disease and harsh working conditions killed off many of them. Young Robert Beale in 1680, for instance, was 'afflicted with the King's Evil' (scrofula, a disease popularly supposed to be curable only on being touched by the King): 'He hath bin gone with his friends about half a year and not likely ever to return,' his master reported—and he did not. Some proved unsuited to the work or found that other work came more easily. In 1672 Cornelius Harbotle reported that his apprentice, Thomas Drew, was 'incapable of learning his trade' and he was sent packing.

That some apprentices were badly treated is shown by the existence of a special procedure whereby complaints between masters and apprentices could be raised before the Chamberlain of London. Young Tom Mitchell complained against his master in 1786 'for not giving him sufficient food, sleeping in the coal hole, not having had clean sheets since last February, repeatedly beating him in a cruel manner and keeping the lad to work from 5 o'clock in the morning till 2 or 3 o'clock next morning'. It was not all one-sided, however. One master complained 'that he suspected his apprentice of an improper familiarity with the nursemaid, she having been found in his bedroom . . .' Of course, this one was not an apprentice clockmaker!

A constant flow of young lads from the provinces was needed to replenish this London wastage, and the flow never faltered. The apprenticeship system, of course, operated also in the provinces, but for a trainee clockmaker in the seventeenth century London was *the* place.

Given that the clockmaker had the most envied of all crafts, let us examine some of the basic problems he faced, for his struggle to overcome them is basically the story of British clockmaking.

A clock in its simplest form consists of a set of interconnected wheels, called a train, pulled round by the force of either a spring or a weight. If there were no means of slowing down the rate at which the wheels rotated they would simply spin round rapidly according to the degree of force imposed by the weight or spring, the clock hands likewise whizzing round the dial. The problem for the early clockmaker was to devise a means of slowing down the pull on the wheels in a way which was capable of fine control and regulation, so that the clock would record the hours and minutes into which we divide the day.

That is all. The rest is simply mathematical ability and engineering skill, both of which clockmakers had at their disposal in far greater measure than we are inclined to realise. Past technology was almost always more advanced than we give credit for. In 1626, for instance, when the famous watchmaker Robert Grinking senior died, he left to his son, Robert junior, 'all my mathematicall bookes, tooles and workinge instruments of my trade'. So they had the mathematics and the technology—design was the missing factor.

Who it was who first devised a system for regulating a clock we do not know, nor does it much matter. It was in the distant dawn of European clockmaking and long before the start of the British craft, so we need worry no further. The device by which clocks were so regulated was called an *escapement*; it allowed power to 'escape' from the tensioned wheel train in a series of regular jerks, a start/stop operation repeated incessantly until the power source ran down. The escapement was the pace-setter, the vital device which held in control all the remaining sections of the clock regardless of how many wheels there were in the train or what their functions may have been. The last wheel in the train, the one which connected with the escapement, was termed the *escapement wheel* or *escape wheel*, which some like to call the *'scape wheel*; just to make things complicated, it is sometimes referred to as the *crown wheel* because it looks a bit like a crown.

The earliest form of escapement is called a *verge escapement*. The verge is simply an upright rod with projections (called pallets) which intermittently get in the way of the escape wheel as it attempts to turn under the pull of the weight or spring. The verge is pushed alternately to the left and right and the time which passes during each alternate swing of the verge is the

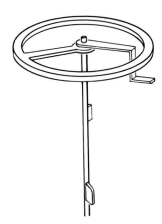

Fig. 1. The balance-wheel regulator, the earliest device used in regulating British household clocks. The wheel is made to rotate alternately to the left and to the right as impulses from the teeth of the escape-wheel (not shown) push against the projecting pallets on the balance-wheel arbor.

pulse-rate of the clock. Without some sort of weight on the verge itself the clock would rattle away like a machine gun. Therefore a weighted arm (called a *foliot*) was attached to the verge—on European clocks. In Britain, however, clockmakers would have nothing to do with the foliot, but instead used a circular weighted arm, rather like a single-spoked steering wheel, called a *balance wheel*. (Figure 1 shows a balance wheel on a verge staff with projecting pallets, which would alternately contact the escape wheel.)

The balance wheel was a satisfactory regulator in the sense that its backward and forward swing did act in the desired manner to slow down the wheel-train speed to a manageable pace, a pace that was exactly determined by the gearing of the wheels. Its big disadvantage was that it had no means of fine adjustment. The only method of making the clock go faster was to add to the driving weight, done by slipping on thin lead washers or by adding lead shot into the hollow at the top of the weight canister. With a spring-driven clock the best you could do was to adjust the tension of the spring. Consequently timekeeping was very imperfect with balance-wheel clocks.

An early writer on clockwork, John Smith, summed up the situation in his book *Horological Dialogues* in 1675, a time when Smith had the advantage of a new means of regulation and could look back at the old-fashioned balance wheel with condescension (and fairly tortured grammar).

These movements [clock language for works] going with weights must be brought to keep true time by adding to or diminishing from them: if they go too slow you must add thin shifts of lead to the weights to make it go faster, but if it go too fast then you must diminish the weight to make it go slower, for that, whensoever you find it to gain or loose, you must thus, by adding or diminishing, rectifie its motion: note that these Ballance movements *are exceedingly subject to be altered by the change of weather*, and therefore are most commonly very troublesome to keep to a true time . . .

Note that important part (the italics are mine) about the weather. Of course, he was not referring to fog, wind or rain, but to variations in temperature, which would particularly affect performance between summer and winter and night and day. Being made largely of brass with a smaller proportion of steel, these clocks were prone to expansion and contraction, which played havoc with the timekeeping. We shall come back to 'weather' later.

Spring-driven clocks were even more of a nuisance to regulate. The pull of a weight is constant, whether the clock is fully wound up or almost run down. A spring, on the other hand, pulls very strongly when fully wound up and loses strength progressively as it runs down. Add to this the factor that spring-making itself was an imperfect process in the seventeeth century. Try hammering a piece of steel into a long thin strip and coiling it so that it can be wound and unwound repeatedly without breaking, and you will see what was involved. The maker of spring-driven clocks was faced with real problems.

An ingenious attempt at solving the inconstant power problem of spring clocks was the fusee or fuzee (figure 2), a cone-shaped drum so fitted that its smaller end, requiring greater pulling force, acted as a drag against the maximum pull of the fully-wound spring. The gut line gradually fed along to meet the wider end of the fusee, which provided less of a drag, when the spring was at its weakest. The fusee was, therefore, a compensation gear to rectify the spring's uneven pull; it was used for over three hundred years.

The maker of spring clocks had, moreover, to get the spring and the fusee inside the box or case of the clock, and both these items were extra to the normal contents of a weight-driven one.

So why bother to make spring clocks when they were beset with all these extra problems not found in weight-driven ones? The answer lay in the fact that spring clocks, being self-contained, were portable. You could move them from one piece of furniture to another, one room to another, one house to another, simply by picking them up. Moving a weight-driven

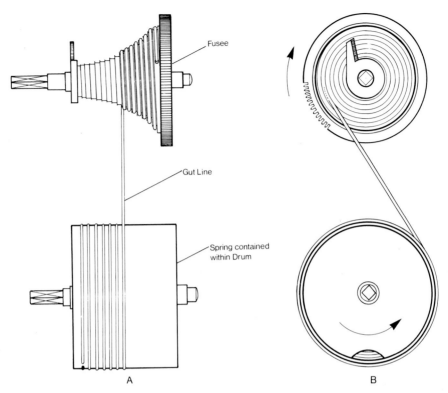

Fusee

Gut Line

Spring contained
within Drum

A   B

Fig. 2. The fusee, seen from the side in *A* and the end in *B*. The fusee was a compensating gear to rectify the variation in the pull of the spring. When fully wound, all the gutline would be coiled on the fusee so that the spring, then at its strongest, found more resistance to turning the fusee, since it was pulling at the gutline wound round the narrow end, than when it was almost run down, when the gutline is wound only around the wider end. Here the clock is half wound.

clock was a much more troublesome affair. A spring clock stood on any flat surface, such as a table.

A development of the spring clock became the watch, the ultimate in portability. You could carry one with you all the time if you wished—if you were wealthy enough you could even carry a pocketful to a tennis match to give away to friends! Such miniaturisation was a real test of skill and the watchmakers gradually formed into a specialised clique of their own.

If accurate timekeeping in larger weight-driven clocks was a problem, then accuracy in smaller spring-driven ones was more so, and accuracy in watches was a nightmare. Despite this, the top men in the craft went in for spring clocks and watches. Why? Not because it offered an intriguing challenge—

though it did. It was because this was what the luxury market demanded. Looking back for a moment to the quotation at the head of this chapter, William's father, when leaving him the watch, bothered to point out that it cost three pounds twelve shillings and was the one 'which I commonly carrie about me' because he was proud of it, proud to be one of the top people who could have a watch to carry around and proud to have paid so highly for it. Three pounds twelve shillings would have paid a labourer's wages for a year. 'You set that down in writing,' William's father would have said to his lawyer: 'the one which cost three pounds twelve shillings.'

What was wanted were watches to show off all day long, spring clocks to scatter on every table, pocketsful of watches for young princes to give away. Money was no object. Ingenuity, skill and time were well rewarded. The man who could make such things *and* make them beautiful to look at and handle, mystifying in their operations, magical in the information they recorded, enchanting in the melodies they played—such a man could expect kings amongst his customers.

David Ramsay is important as being the first known Briton to achieve fame in this field. He was a Scot, believed to have come from Dundee. Whatever part of Scotland he came from, his horological skills were decidedly French in nature. The few watches and one clock of his which survive are distinctly French in manner, and it is known that he spent time in France. His son, William, wrote that 'when James I succeeded to the crown of England he sent into France for my father, who was there . . .' and James made him 'keeper of his Majesty's clocks and watches'.

Ramsay's journeyman in 1622 was William Pettit, an 'alien' whose occasional use of his real name of Guillaume betrays his French origins. Pettit worked at Tutle Street (?Tothill Street) in Westminster and was still there in 1662, styled specifically as a boxmaker, which was one who made the 'boxes' for watches; i.e., watch cases. A boxmaker, of course, may well also have made the boxes or cases for early table clocks, such as the one known to be by Ramsay. Pettit's skill as an engraver and worker in precious metals is illustrated in his gift in 1655 of a silver boat to the Clockmakers' Company, who were most pleased to accept, having met with precious little success over the preceding twenty-five years in their attempts at extracting financial contributions from him. I mention Pettit because it seems highly likely that he did the work for which Ramsay took the glory. The French style of Ramsay's work is not surprising if it was executed by a Frenchman.

Ramsay was obviously a court favourite, for he was given all manner of court sinecures, fees, pensions—in fact the variety of excuses under which he was given royal monies is ingenious to say the least. He seems to have been a human dynamo, his fertile mind alive with invention. Records show him as a student of the occult sciences, experimenting with divining rods, inventor of a new process for melting copper, another to make hard iron soft, an engine to drain coal mines, a process for making saltpetre, one for separating gold from impure metals, fire-hose pumps, weaving looms, fertilisers . . . Did he really invent all these, or was he getting the credit for them by presenting news of such discoveries to the Royal ear? Contemporary records describe him as 'not a man on whose discretion to rely, being much transported with self-opinion'. As if his duties as Page of the Bedchamber were not enough on top of his other interests, not only was he responsible for supplying clocks and watches for the crown but also he had custody of the numerous royal horological treasures. It is hardly surprising if he were self-opinionated.

I do not believe for one minute that Ramsay sat patiently engraving watches. He was an inventor and metallurgist with court connections and royal patronage, a busy man about town. He lived 'within two doors of the Wounded Hart in Holborn', which must have been convenient for him.

When the Clockmakers' Company was formed in 1631, Ramsay was appointed its first Master, a task which he seems to have regarded about as seriously as his other sinecures, as he attended barely one meeting in twenty years, and that for the purpose of extracting a grant for himself. He was known in the Company as Squire Ramsay.

These were troubled times. Ramsay's apparent loyalty to his royal benefactors is illustrated when in 1661, just over a year after his death, his widow was given a grant of £600 as compensation for her distress under the Commonwealth, having been 'plundered for raising a troop of horse for the late King at her own charge'. The way the royal monies flowed like water in Ramsay's direction contrasts very sharply with the official fee paid to Randolph Bull as Royal Clockmaker—one shilling a day. Ramsay may not have found the philosopher's stone, but it certainly seems as if most things that he touched turned into gold just the same.

Ramsay is important as the first Briton to make himself a niche in this French-dominated craft. However, he achieved this not by beating the French but by joining them. The work which bore his Scottish name was still French literally and in style, the difference being that in charge of it all was if not an Englishman, then the next best thing, a Scot.

The first half-century of British clockmaking passed with Europeans, principally Frenchmen, still dominating the craft. It was this domination by 'aliens' which led a group of sixteen disgruntled so-called British craftsmen to band together against the common enemy in an attempt to petition the King for a charter to form their own Company of Clockmakers. This took place in 1622 and met with no success. It is a reflection of the small scale of the trade at this time that these sixteen men could claim to be the complete British contingent and that the total workforce in the capital, foreigners included, was under sixty in number—and that included apprentices and journeyman as well as masters. If we analyse the names of petitioners and aliens we arrive at a maximum of only thirty business houses where clocks or watches were made.

Of the forty-one aliens, all but two were either known Frenchmen or had French names. Of the 'British' petitioners four of the sixteen are themselves believed to have been of recent French origin, and one of them (Ferdinando Garret) was actually employing as his journeymen two of the very foreigners complained against. Robert Grinkin the elder, one of the ringleaders, was an important figure in the Blacksmiths' Company, and some of the other signatories can be traced as his former apprentices and journeymen. The petitioners were really the Grinkin company, and it was to some extent a case of London-resident Frenchmen taking exception to newly-arrived Frenchmen stealing what the former regarded as their own monopoly trade—the British market. It is not surprising that products of this period have a French flavour.

If we consider such works as are known by these fifty-seven men, foreigners and so-called British, we find that many were known makers of watches and by one is known a table clock, but by only one is known an English weight-driven clock—a lantern clock by Francis Foreman.

But, remarkable as it may seem from the circumstances, by the 1620s there were signs of the beginning of a native British craft. French clocks were mostly of the spring-driven type, and like watches were aimed purely at the luxury market which the Frenchmen had nicely cornered. There was hardly anyone catering for the potentially much wider market of cheaper clocks, those of the simpler weight-driven type known today as lantern clocks. It was on this market that the first truly British school of clockmakers set their sights.

2 *Lantern Clocks*

Here lieth little Samuel Barrington that great undertaker
Of famous cities clock and chime maker;
He made his own time to go early and later,
But now he's returned to God his Creator.
The 19th November then he ceas'd,
And for his memory this is here plac'd.

BY HIS SON BEN *1693.*
(Epitaph from a tombstone.)

The English lantern clock—its alternative names now and then—its styles and periods—its three types of regulator—winged versions—how to set it by the sundial and the Equation of Time—Turkish models—regions of manufacture and distribution—travellers' models—sheep's-heads and birdcages—the lantern family tree

In figure 3 we have a typical all-metal hanging weight-driven wall clock called a lantern clock, the first truly British form of clock. With their larger, coarser wheelwork, lantern clocks have their origins in the native turret-clockmaking/locksmithing/blacksmithing tradition in which a good many British makers were schooled; the French-inspired watch and spring-clock craft was of an altogether more delicate nature.*

---

* The Clockmakers' Company ultimately served to fuse two schools into one, but for long after the formation of the Company many of these heavier metalworkers remained within the auspices of the Blacksmiths' Company even though they were clockmakers, not blacksmiths. This early link between clockmaking and locksmith work can be seen clearly in the rules of the Edinburgh clockmakers' guild, the Incorporation of Hammermen. To qualify for admission an applicant had to make a test-piece, as with the Clockmakers' Company, but in Edinburgh he had to make not only a clock but also a lock and key.

No one knows when or how the name 'lantern clock' originated, though it is generally supposed to have arisen through the clock's similarity to a lantern. A recently popular suggestion that it may have derived from a mispronunciation of 'latten clock' is ingenious and some writers now proclaim it as if it were fact; but while latten was brass-like it was not the same thing as brass, and the word was never used simply to mean brass.

While the term 'lantern clock' may be quite modern in origin, we do know what such clocks were called in the early seventeenth century when they were the *only* weight-driven clocks and there would be little possibility of confusion. We can even quote examples.

In 1642 the Clockmakers' Company gave a *chamber clock* to the Painter Stainers' Company for being allowed use of their hall. In that same year William Bowyer gave the Company a *great chamber clock* (i.e., a large one) for excusal from all future offices. In 1652 John Pennock gave the Company a *house clock*. That same year Company officers confiscated a badly made *chamber clock* from Samuel Davis' shop in Lothbury. In 1653 John Almond brought to the Company *a good substantial house clock* as evidence of his abilities. I chose these examples as, being before 1658, they must obviously have been pre-pendulum balance-wheel lantern clocks, apparently known then as house clocks or chamber clocks.

While those in the trade used the correct terminology, the ordinary person would often refer to a lantern clock simply as a clock; there was only one kind of household clock and he had no need to qualify his description. On occasions, however, the man in the street chose to call them brass clocks— we know this from the evidence of old inventories.

We must remember that the spring-driven clock was prohibitively expensive and therefore not a common type of clock. Most people would never have seen one, let alone owned one. Even in spite of the very high survival rate of items belonging to the nobility, we know British spring-driven table clocks of balance-wheel type through only a handful of surviving examples, and this is an indication of how very few were made.

Some take exception to the term 'Cromwellian clock', by which lantern clocks are sometimes known—yet many of these same people are content to live with the totally misleading expressions 'bracket clock' to describe clocks that have nothing to do with brackets, 'Act of Parliament clocks' that have nothing to do with Acts of Parliament, 'sheepshead' clocks that have nothing to do with sheep or heads, and Grandfather and Grandmother clocks that have no special relevance to elderly members of the family!

Plate 1. Provincial balance-wheel lantern clock signed 'Tho:Tue deL'inn fecit Dece'br ye: 5th 1663' (made in Kings Lynn). It apparently had alarmwork originally but this is now missing. The alarm setting-disc would have covered the plain centre area of the dial, hiding the signature, which is presently visible. The clock stands sixteen inches high. The maker died in 1710 aged 97.

Plate 2. Rear view of the Thomas Tue lantern clock showing countwheel mechanism and original balance-wheel control. The shaped pillars, feet and finials can be seen clearly as well as their connection with the top and bottom plates.

I do not wish to defend the term 'Cromwellian clocks', but I find it odd that no one has a good word to say for it. I cannot help but wonder whether it might be that, the restoration of the monarchy in 1660 coinciding with the introduction of the new longcase clock, hostile anti-Cromwellian attitudes looked back disdainfully at the now old-fashioned lantern clock as an object from those unenlightened times and gave it the derogatory political label of 'Cromwellian'. In just the same way, antique dealers have until quite recently disparaged anything 'Victorian' until the very term came to signify all that was ugly and undesirable in the antique world. Indeed, we still belittle the Victorian longcase clocks as being badly designed, as though we were in a better position to judge than the people who made them. It is incredible conceit. Lantern clocks *were* made before the Interregnum (1642–1660), but not that many of them, and they *were* made after the Restoration, but in steadily decreasing numbers and frequently as a known anachronism that happened to be conveniently portable; so it is not unrealistic to see the lantern clock as a child of the Interregnum, and if we use the term 'Cromwellian clock' there is no possible doubt as to the type of clock signified. But we would be frowned upon in horological circles!

By 1620 the English lantern clock had taken on its definitive shape. Gradually more lantern-clockmakers began to appear—though we are still talking in terms of only a handful. The average height of these clocks was about fourteen or fifteen inches, though miniature ones about six or seven inches high exist. The zenith of lantern-clock making was in the period 1640–1660.

There is an important feature about all lantern clocks from this early period which facilitates recognition of them regardless of evidence in the form of stylistics (which we will shortly look at in any event): they were all controlled by the balance wheel, until about 1655–1658, when the pendulum was introduced. This has certain consequences which greatly assist us in identification, even if the clock has been modified or converted since.

Early lantern clocks had a separate rope for each train, one for the going train at the front of the clock, one for the striking train at the back; some had, additionally, one for alarm work. The lantern clock therefore had two separate weights each independent of the other, and the clock might have a duration of from eight to twelve hours at each winding, depending on how high it was hung on the wall. There is evidence which suggests they were hung as close to the ceiling as possible, rather than at head height, which we might today think of as usual.

Fig. 3. Typical outline and detail of a lantern clock, this one dating from the mid-seventeenth century and made by John Buck, who is known to have lived in Chester in the 1660s. Note the tulip-style engraving in the dial centre, the dolphin frets and the simple hour hand, all of which are highly typical of the period.

Many of these short-duration rope systems may later have been modified to take the Huygens 'endless rope' system as used on thirty-hour longcase clocks, in order to gain the benefit of a full thirty-hour run. But that does not concern us here. The fact that the early ones had two distinctly separate weights meant that the internal wheel layout had to be such that both weights did not travel down at the same side of the clock. Apart from possibly fouling together, such a one-sided distribution of the weights would have pulled the clock askew on its hook. Therefore, as technicalities dictated that the going weight must fall on the left of the clock, the strike weight had to fall on the right and so the bell hammer had to be positioned also on the right (as seen when facing the clock dial). What could be easier to recognise? A right-hand bell hammer indicates a balance-wheel controlled lantern clock, which probably dates from before 1657; only a few were made with balance wheel after 1657.

Other features of a stylistic rather than technical nature indicate an early lantern clock. Narrow chapter rings with short stumpy numbers and a simple motif between numbers preceded wider chapter rings with much taller numbers and more elaborate motifs. The early chapter ring just overlapped the upright pillars at the sides while later ones projected well past the pillars; this broader type is often known as a 'sheep's-head' clock, presumably because someone with poor eyesight or a well-developed sense of imagination saw in it a likeness to the head of a sheep. Early seventeenth-century lantern clocks have a double engraved band outside the hour numbers; later chapter rings have a single band.

The finials and feet of early lantern clocks are slim with multiple turnings; later ones have more rounded, simpler feet. The style of fret is said by some to identify the period and by others to have no bearing on period: the front fret is frequently engraved while the side frets are left plain; some authorities maintain that engraved side-frets are an indication of the pre-1660 period. It is worth mentioning that frets are frequently replacements and hence unreliable for dating. A happy compromise in using frets for dating would seem to be to suggest that some help and some do not. For instance, the double dolphin fret seems to have been popular over a long period and therefore is not particularly helpful in indicating age. The coat-of-arms fret, however, seems to have been used mostly in the early period, say 1640–1660. An unusual version has the lion and unicorn for supporters, but more commonly the shield is within scrollwork. A common pattern has meaningless leafwork design, said to represent tulips, and this appears both early and late.

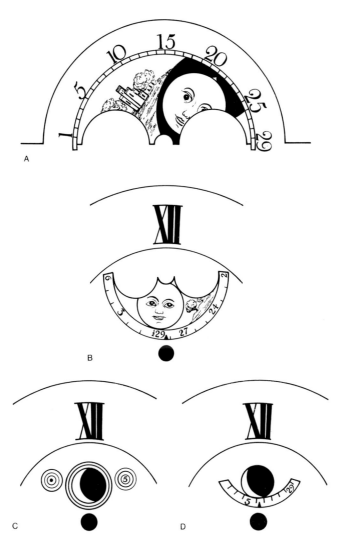

Fig. 4. Moons. *A*: The normal type of moon dial as found in the arch on both brass and japanned dials from about 1750 to 1850. The moonwheel itself is painted in either instance. It is known as an arch moon or sometimes as a rolling moon. *B*: A twelve-o'clock moon, devised as a manner of incorporating a moon dial into a square-dial clock. This type of moon dial appears commonly on japanned dials from about 1780 to 1840, but also occasionally on brass dials as early as about 1770. The moonwheel itself is painted in either instance. *C* and *D*: two types of twelve-o'clock moon dial found on brass-dial clocks from about 1720 to about 1750. The moonwheel in each instance is of brass and shows through a hole in the dial. These types are often known as a halfpenny moon (or, occasionally, a penny moon) or a Halifax moon, the latter term arising from the fact that this feature was very popular in that area and indeed in the north of England in general.

One uncommon type of lantern clock has 'wings'; that is, projecting flanges at either side. These were conceived in the short-pendulum period, strictly after 1658 and before about 1675, although, as the short pendulum was still used in lantern clocks for a considerable time after the introduction of the long pendulum, this does not mean that a winged lantern clock would necessarily have been made between those dates. With these clocks the (short) pendulum swings between the two trains, and, probably because of the lack of space for the normal pendulum 'bob', the pendulum has the shape of an anchor, one barb of which projects at each swing.

The hands of lantern clocks developed in style over the years and can assist in identification of period, provided the clock has the original single hand; while some lantern clocks do have two hands, this is usually because minute-work has been added later (a feature which may sometimes be given away by the absence of minute markings on the chapter ring). Very few, if any, early lantern clocks are accepted as having been made with two hands—with inaccuracy in timekeeping of pre-pendulum clocks amounting to ten minutes a day or more, what point was there in showing minutes? Accuracy to the nearest quarter-hour was as much as one might hope for, or have need for; accordingly, the divisions on the chapter rings represented hours, half-hours and quarter-hours.

Let us not forget that there was no accurate means even of setting the clock in the first place. The only method was to dash outside and see what the sundial told you. Supposing you *had* a sundial and supposing it marked units of less than a quarter-hour, and supposing the dial divisions were engraved with absolute precision, and supposing the sun were shining, and supposing you were to read it accurately—even if one allows optimum conditions (which in reality would not apply), then you still had the problem that the sun did not tell you the right time anyway!

The reason for this is explained by what is dauntingly described as the Equation of Time. For convenience we divide the day into twenty-four hours, and clocks were therefore made to show these twenty-four hours each day and every day. However, if we measure the time each day at which the sun is exactly overhead we find that it is *not* exactly at noon. The sun is some days a little early and some days a little late. The reason is that the orbit of the earth round the sun is not a true circle but an ellipse. The sun is consistent and does follow a set timetable, but not the artificial twenty-four-hours-a-day timetable that man devised for it. A sundial reading will therefore be consistently *in*accurate by our twenty-four-hours-a-day time, which we call *mean* time. The degree of what we impertinently call the sun's inaccuracy is calculable, and in the past was sometimes engraved as additional information on a sundial or supplied as a printed sheet with a new clock so that it could be set to mean time by using a sundial and this 'equation table'. An interesting addendum to an advertisement of one MacPherson, an Edinburgh clockmaker, appeared in the *Caledonian Mercury* in 1783: 'N.B. At the said shop and nowhere else may be had equation tables, without which no gentleman or watchmaker can set clocks or watches with the sundial.' Such tables might show that the sun was fast by over sixteen minutes at certain times of year or slow by over fourteen minutes at other times. On four widely separated days in the year solar time and mean time coincide; at all other times they differ.

It sounds incredibly conceited for mankind to regard his own timekeepers as more accurate than the time kept by the sun, although for man's own purposes this is true. This 'inaccuracy' of the sun is the basis for that 'traditional' rhyme which runs:

> *There's the cottage of Peter,*
> *That cunning old fox,*
> *Who kept the sun right*
> *By the time of his clocks.*

This is supposed to have been said in the later eighteenth century of the clockmaker Peter Clare of Manchester by his neighbours. Whether or not you believe that eighteenth-century people were more inclined to chant rhymes about their neighbours than we are today, it is interesting that the clockmaker had not only to make clocks which ran accurately but also to educate the public at large to the fact that his clocks were accurate and the sun really was 'wrong'.

The Equation of Time is relevant to lantern clocks in two respects. Firstly, it appears that the first equation tables were not printed until after the invention of the pendulum, probably because there was little point in correcting your lantern clock by three minutes from the sundial time if it would lose at least that degree of accuracy over the next few hours. Secondly, the nation at large was working purely on solar time in these early prependulum days, and therefore had no means of timing a clock 'accurately' anyway as far as ordinary domestic use was concerned. For long after clocks that indicated mean time had come into use many people would still set them by the sundial. As solar time varied in different parts of the country, there was no uniform time throughout the land. To talk of accuracy in terms of minutes in these conditions is foolishness.

A pre-pendulum lantern clock with two hands, therefore, hardly seems credible, though we ought not to rule out the possibility that an occasional clockmaker may have been contrary enough to make one.

Let us return briefly to the style of the single hand. Early ones are said to resemble an arrowhead, by which it is meant that they are simple, slender yet sturdy, and with the business end symmetrically shaped. The single hand had a tail, a straight continuation, to assist one in leverage when gripping the hand to reset the time. Later hands have more ornate pointers tending to a heart or ace-of-spades shape with more piercings.

Some clockmakers were quick to take advantage of the world supremacy which the British craft attained in the later seventeenth century, giving rise as it did to a considerable demand from overseas for British clocks and watches. In particular, the Middle Eastern market seems to have been an attractive one and lantern clocks were made specifically for this area. We call these 'Turkish' lantern clocks, as the numerals on them look very Turkish to Europeans with no knowledge of that language. This type of lantern clock often has an arched dial rather like a miniature longcase dial. Spandrels and hands on these clocks often have a Turkish look about them as opposed to conventional English styles.

Turkish market lantern clocks, which usually have the short bob pendulum, were made from about 1680, although most are eighteenth-century. They continued to be made long after the English lantern clock had passed away, even into the nineteenth century. They were mostly made by London makers: the names of Christopher Gould, Markwick Markham, Isaac Rodgers and George Prior come to mind amongst those well known for their Turkish output—though not only in lantern clocks. Other sorts of clocks and watches were made for the Turkish market, but it is principally the lantern clocks that one notices: Turkish lanterns stand out by their anachronistic retention of the old bob pendulum long after its inadequacies had been recognised.

This brings us to the question of the distribution of lantern clocks. It was a trade which began essentially in London. There *are* provincial examples before about 1660 but they are very few. In the later seventeenth century provincial output increased considerably, probably more or less in proportion to the waning of the London market, but this provincial increase was limited to certain areas only, namely those where the London influence had been strongest and where London-trained men migrated to seek new markets —Essex, for instance, and Suffolk, Norfolk, the Home Counties and the southern Midlands. Bristol and Bath formed a small nucleus for West Country work, as Edinburgh did for Scotland (though this was a special case which we shall look at shortly).

But what about the other areas? Where are all the lantern clocks made in Cornwall–Devon–Dorset, Staffordshire–Cheshire–Lancashire, the Lake counties, Yorkshire or Northumberland? I cannot trace a single example of a lantern clock of Welsh or Irish make. There are whole vast regions where the lantern clock was virtually unknown. In many of the remoter counties there is a great scarcity of examples, with the few that are known being often by London-trained men who moved there. Why? Because clockmaking in these areas did not really get under way until after the invention of the pendulum, the long pendulum even, by which time the lantern clock as a form had already become outmoded, replaced by the far more sensible thirty-hour *cased* clock.

It is interesting to uncover what we can of lantern-clock making in Scotland; it does not take long. If we exclude David Ramsay, then the first Scottish maker of clocks other than turret clocks was Humphrey Mills, also sometimes styled Humphrey Milne (*milne* being the Scottish form of *mill*). His work is known through only four or five examples, and these are lantern clocks of the London type. Although Mills himself is believed to have been English (his nephew and successor was from Staffordshire), this does not alter the fact that what are apparently the only lantern clocks of Scottish make bear the name of Humphrey Mills of Edinburgh.

At first sight it would appear, therefore, that a small school of lantern-clock making sprang up in Edinburgh, though it was apparently short-lived. It was in fact a one-man school. But when we look at a Humphrey Mills lantern clock there is something inconsistent between the fine workmanship of the clock and the appallingly crude and uneven punch-lettering of his name on the fret. It suggests at the very least that Mills could not engrave, for the man who could engrave the beautiful floral pattern of a lantern-clock dial centre would never mar his work by such crude punch lettering.

This is not intended to be a condemnation of Mills for his inability to engrave. Engraving was a specialist aspect of the trade and a good many makers who were superb at making clocks were not only unable to engrave, but some could not even write their own names. It is quite wrong to imagine, as is sometimes stated, that the Clockmakers' Company ensured that every maker could perform all the various tasks of the trade. In any case, that Company had no jurisdiction away from the capital. So who did Humphrey Mills' engraving on the dials?

Humphry Mills

— *Edvardus East Londini* —

Fig. 5. *Above,* an example of lettering applied by hammer and individual single-letter punches. This illustration, copied exactly from a Humphrey Mills lantern clock of the late seventeenth century, shows clearly the careless nature of the work, a sharp contrast with the 'signature' (*below*) on an Edward East clock of the same period, which is an example of skilled engraving. The style of engraved signature with which a man usually signed his work was for effect, and frequently bore little resemblance to the handwritten signature of the same person.

Here is an interesting set of coincidences. Young Edmund Appley died in 1688 aged about thirty-one. He was a London clockmaker at Charing Cross known to have made lantern clocks, having been apprenticed to Jeffrey Bayley, also known for lantern clocks, who in turn had been trained by Thomas Pace, again known for lantern clocks. Now Appley died *in Edinburgh*, as he explained in his hastily conceived will, 'having come to Scotland about necessary affairs and there falling sick and fearing that my sickness be unto death . . .'—he was right! An executor to the will of this unfortunate man, dying away from home among strangers, was Andrew Brown, clock-maker of Edinburgh. Andrew very kindly paid for the church bells to be rung at Appley's funeral on 11 August 1688. This Andrew Brown was none other than a former apprentice of Humphrey Mills, and in 1688 he was almost certainly employed as journeyman to Mills.

In Edmund Appley, therefore, we have a known London lantern-clock maker in contact with the only known Edinburgh maker of lantern clocks, a man who could not engrave his own name. It does not require a great stretch of the imagination to wonder whether Appley was selling lantern clocks to Mills for the latter to 'sign' with his own crude punch lettering.

32

If this assumption is correct, it would explain why the Edinburgh lantern-clock school was restricted to the work of one man.

Mills died about 1692, after which Andrew Brown carried on making, not lantern clocks, but longcase ones. And of course the lantern-clock trade was very much on the wane by this time in Great Britain as a whole, being thereafter restricted to the small travelling alarm versions and the provincial sheep's-head types.

The relevance of this provincial distribution will emerge shortly. But first let us recap a little. As time progressed the lantern clock developed in several directions. With the arrival of the pendulum, the new short-pendulum principle was applied. Within a very few years the improved long pendulum, with its much more accurate timekeeping, was adopted. This meant that, by the 1680s, there were three types of lantern clocks still in production. First there was the old balance-wheel type, though presumably now made in very small numbers or for special reasons—e.g., its more easy portability. Secondly there was the short-pendulum type. And thirdly there was the long (or Royal) pendulum type with anchor escapement; even though the anchor escapement required a much more precise 'level' position than either the balance-wheel or short-pendulum versions, and even though this escapement was not designed for lantern clocks with all their encumbrances of dangling pendulum and weights, yet still the old 'Cromwellian' lantern clock was produced.

Why? What on earth was the point, when the thirty-hour longcase clock did everything that the lantern clock could do, and did it better and probably at no greater expense? We don't know, except in one respect: the travelling alarm type of lantern clock used when journeying away from home, often provided with a small wooden carrying case, would obviously have been impractical with a pendulum about thirty inches long. These clocks were smaller than the normal versions—usually about eight or nine inches high.

As to the ordinary household lantern clock, there can have been only one reason—that it was a well loved form of clock—because it continued only in those areas where it had formerly been popular. When we think of 'late' examples, dating from about 1700 to about 1750, even occasionally later, what areas of the country are we thinking of? Not London, but really only East Anglia—Essex, Suffolk, Norfolk, the traditional lantern-clock region. One can quote an occasional provincial maker elsewhere who was an exception, but he is only a *very* occasional one. Lantern-clock land was the south-eastern corner of England. Therefore, when we refer to the late type of lantern clock commonly known as a sheep's-head type, we are thinking particularly of clocks from this area; in fact, some authorities define a sheep's-head as being a lantern clock from East Anglia.

The popularity of the lantern clock in south-eastern England and its virtual absence from the north and west is the root cause of two other distinct differences in clockwork between these regions.

One is that, while the lantern clock developed in its own area into the birdcage thirty-hour longcase (otherwise known as the post-framed movement), in the north-west, where there was no lantern tradition, the thirty-hour longcase began life as Huygens had designed it, namely as a plate-framed movement like the eight-day one.

The second difference stems from the fact that the lantern clock was a *wall clock*, hanging from some convenient hook by its iron hoop, and steadied and held out from the wall by two iron spurs behind its back feet.

The south-eastern tradition called for a hanging wall-clock, and in these regions, even after the demise of the lantern clock, the fondness for a hanging clock was still catered for by its successor, the birdcage hooded clock. In the north-west, where there was no hanging-clock tradition, hooded clocks are very much rarer—indeed you would have difficulty finding any example from some of the north-western counties.

In the south-eastern areas the family tree of the lantern clock reads something like this: The lantern gave birth to the sheep's-head, some hoop and spike versions, some standing on wall brackets. Some lantern clocks adopted the dial type of the ordinary longcase clock and became square-dial or arched-dial wall clocks with a lantern movement, both hoop and spike versions and those that stood on wall brackets. Some took on the developed birdcage movement with square or arched dial, with or without hoop and spikes, with or without wall brackets. Somewhere along the line emerged the option of having a completely enclosed wooden hood (or head as they then called it) and one might find almost any of these combinations developing into a full hooded clock form. These were almost all transitory stages, for the only type which continued in unbroken line was the ordinary thirty-hour birdcage longcase clock.

What a complicated group of interrelated clocks! In the north-west life was much simpler, with just the one type of thirty-hour plated longcase clock. Of course, there were eight-day clocks in all these areas, but in all areas an eight-day longcase clock was just exactly that, and from the start was a plated movement with no permutations.

Between 1700 and 1750 the thirty-hour longcase clock undoubtedly took over from the lantern clock as the dominant type, even in the south-east. However, as the lantern clock dwindled in popularity some of the hybrid wall and hooded clocks had short periods of favour. It may not be irrelevant that the eastern areas where the hooded clocks flourished also happened to be those areas closest to Holland, where too, the hooded wall clock was a popular type.

Plate 3. Dial of thirty-hour single-handed clock by John Fletcher of Ripponden, *c.* 1730.

3 *The Pendulum*

There is lately a way found out for making of clocks that go exact and keep equaller time than any now made . . . Made by Ahasuerus Fromanteel, who made the first that were in England.

(Advertisement of Ahasuerus Fromanteel in 1658.)

———◆———

The Clockmakers' Company is formed—maladministration and discontent—Ahasuerus Fromanteel—Huygens—the short pendulum—the Coster contract—Cromwell and political factors—the anchor escapement and long pendulum—William Clement—Joseph Knibb—the dead-beat escapement—George Graham—John Harrison

On 22 August 1631 a Charter of Incorporation was granted for the formation of the Clockmakers' Company. The first Master by Royal decree was, predictably, David Ramsay—though in fact he scarcely ever bothered to attend its meetings. The first Wardens and Assistants, who formed the governing body, consisted largely of the Grinkin clan, though Robert Grinkin himself had died five years before and Robert junior was as yet too young to be admitted.

The Company could and did control the practice of the craft in London, the taking of apprentices and the quality of goods manufactured. It had the power to exact financial contributions from the membership and to fine members who infringed the rules. Some authorities write about the 'honour' of being admitted into the Company, as though admission were a sign of a clockmaker's status. This shows a complete misunderstanding of the situation—except that entry was a mark of capability in so far as it proved that a man had served his time and was a competent workman. But that of course applied to very many makers who lived far enough afield to be outside the jurisdiction of the Company, whose authority was limited to the London area. Moreover it is very evident from studying the records that a great many makers regarded it as anything but an honour to be forced to join this completely closed shop.

All this could only lead to great resentment on the part of those clockmakers who were at odds with the administration. From the very formation of the Company there were passionate and violent arguments. In 1633 Lewis Cooke, a clockmaker from York, was made to eat his 'uncivil words' by offering a public apology to John Harris, one of the Wardens, who had criticised Cooke's workmanship. Cooke had promptly called him a liar and told him 'he was a botcher and that he never made so good a peece of work in his life as that was which he found fault with . . .' John Drake, a maker of locks (sic) and watches, also had to apologise for his 'intemperate and disgraceful speeches' on more than one occasion. In 1654 when he was made to pay fifteen years' arrears of subscription, he revealed his Anglo-Saxon background in his choice of four-letter words with which to describe the Master. John Nicasius, the watchmaker, had the distinction of abusing more Masters than anyone else, for which he was repeatedly fined, and although the Court tried to make allowances for 'his temper, too well known to all persons of the Court', he was eventually banned from the Company in 1679, largely at the instigation of Henry Jones, one of those offended, until such time as he apologised—which he never did.

The Company was run in its early years by the Grinkin clan, though now that the elder Grinkin was dead, it was headed by Edward East (Master 1645 and 1653), Simon Bartram (Master 1650 and 1651), the younger Robert Grinkin (Master 1648 and 1654) and John Nicasius (Master 1653 and 1656). This small group, bound together by ties of relationships, friendships, apprenticeships, and perhaps also by politics, controlled the Company by electing each other to the higher offices in rotation. Small wonder that the lower ranks complained, though with no effect.

Another source of discontent was that many Company members had been, and still were, freemen of the Blacksmiths' Company and to a lesser extent of other Companies too. With the demand from the Clockmakers' Company for total allegiance in the form of payment of subscriptions, binding of apprentices, attending of meetings, etc. clashing with the very same demands for loyalty from the Blacksmiths' Company and other Companies, those members trapped between the two were in an impossible situation, constantly threatened with lawsuits, prosecutions and blacklistings.

Eventually the membership rebelled against this maladministration and in 1656 thirty-three of them brought matters into the open by complaining to the Lord Mayor in a petition. They were headed by Ahasuerus Fromanteel and his son-in-law, Thomas Loomes, both of whom belonged to the native English school of weight-driven clockmaking as opposed to the French spring-clock and watch school of the Clockmakers' Company administration. Indeed, one of their chief complaints was that, although the Company was formed to keep out foreigners, yet Frenchmen were 'admitted to rule the Freemen'. The East–Grinkin clan attempted to justify what they claimed was their enforcement of the rules, though the best they could do was to muster the support of a mere fourteen members, who themselves were mostly tied to the administrators by bonds of self-interest. This crisis period in the history of the Clockmakers' Company came in the years between 1655 and 1658. It cannot be coincidence that this three-year period was the very time when British clockmaking was undergoing changes of the most vital importance. The man at the centre of these developments was Ahasuerus Fromanteel.

Fromanteel was the most important clockmaker ever to work in this country, yet ten years ago virtually nothing was known about his life. Indeed, so confused was the Fromanteel background that some books assert that four different Ahasuerus Fromanteels were responsible for the one man's work. Well, there were not four of him, only one, although his work was continued in Holland by his son of the same name. Similarly, many older books list people like Louis Fromanteel, who never existed but was born of one man's misreading of a word, which was copied by others. Dr R. Plomp went a long way towards solving the Fromanteel mysteries, publishing his findings in *Antiquarian Horology* in September 1971. My own researches brought our biographical knowledge to its present state in 1975 (*Antiquarian Horology*, Vol IX, No 2), including such details as his birth at Norwich in February 1607 and his death in 1693 in London. To this day, however, new books appear giving information on the Fromanteels that is totally incorrect. (A more detailed account than that which follows may be found in *Country Clocks and their London Origins*.)

It is extremely important that we remember Fromanteel because he is *the* most important man in the history of British clocks. Others may have improved, embellished or refined his innovations, but what Fromanteel alone achieved set the pattern for British clocks for the best part of three centuries.

We have already seen that all English timekeepers were controlled by the balance-wheel principle, whether driven by weights, as with the native English lantern clock, or by springs, as with the French-born luxury table-clock and the watch. Ahasuerus Fromanteel was almost certainly trained in the traditional English blacksmith/turret clockmaker tradition, though we do not yet know who his master was. We do know that he moved from Norwich to London in 1629, and at the age of twenty-two he must have been only recently released from his apprenticeship. He is recorded in contemporary documents as being a maker of turret clocks by 1630, though no recognisable example seems to survive. It is known that he made balance-wheel lantern clocks of the English 'school', and it seems likely that these formed much of his output for the first twenty-five years of his working life.

In the 1650s interesting developments began to happen in the clock world as the pendulum was first applied to clockwork in place of the old balance-wheel regulator (and in Europe, of course, in place of the foliot). The argument about how far Galileo progressed with his pendulum experiments has been going on since just after he died in 1642, and there is no point in adding to the mystery by repeating at length the confusions of others. Whether Galileo did successfully apply the pendulum to the clock, or whether Dr Robert Hooke did so, as he always claimed, the fact remains that it was Christian Huygens in Holland who first took for himself the credit for evolving this technique.

Even if I were capable of going into the niceties of geometrical calculation to demonstrate how Huygens made his pendulum clocks work, we could be in danger of wallowing in a text resembling the deliberately ill-worded advertisement of George Smith Green, who in 1758 obviously heeded the advice given many of us at school never to use one short Anglo-Saxon word when two long Latinate ones would do just as well, for his advertisement in the *Oxford Journal* for spring and weight clocks read: 'At the Automaton Laboratory Confronting the Portal of All Souls College in Oxford are fabricated and renovated Trochiliack Horloges, portable or permanent, Linguaculous or taciturnal: whose circumgyrations are performed by internal spiral Elastics, or external pendulous Plumbages: Diminutives simple or compound in Aurum, or Argent Intiguments.' With such an advertisement he deserved to sell them!

Huygens simply switched the verge staff on its side into a horizontal position. This meant that the escape wheel had also to rotate in a horizontal plane, which was brought about by means of an intermediate wheel, called

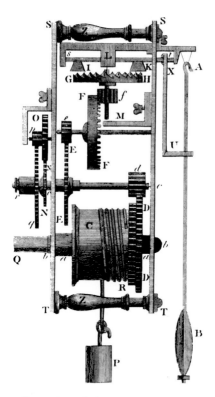

Fig. 6. A contemporary illustration of the verge escapement with short pendulum. The weight, *P*, pulls on the wheels, forcing the crown wheel, *GH*, to impulse the pallets, *I* and *K*, which cause the crutch, *XU*, to swing, thus rocking the short pendulum, *AB*, from side to side, thereby determining the speed at which the wheels are allowed to turn. Notice the finely shaped baluster pillars, *Z*.

a contrate wheel. (Fig. 6 shows this principle.)

The pendulum hung down through a slotted piece of steel, called a crutch, which was attached to the verge staff. (The verge staff is normally called the escape-wheel arbor when used with the later anchor escapement.) Instead of pushing a balance wheel back and forth as a regulator, Huygens' verge staff (through the crutch) now pushed the pendulum from side to side. Since the pendulum could be lengthened or shortened by means of a nut below its little 'bob', fine adjustment could be brought to bear to affect its rate of swing. Shortening the pendulum by raising the bob would make the clock go faster, lengthening it by lowering the bob made it go slower. Because the pendulum swings equally from one side to another its rate of swing is said to be isochronous. Such inventions always look so simple, *after* someone has invented them!

Plate 4. Tiny eight-and-a-half inch dial of the first kind of longcase clock, this one signed below the chapter ring by Ahasuerus Fromanteel, the first man to make these clocks in Britain. It dates from *c.* 1670. The shutters closing the winding holes indicate that this clock has maintaining power, as many of these earliest ones did.

Let us come back at this point to Ahasuerus Fromanteel. Unfortunately for him he chose to follow the anti-Royalist politics of Oliver Cromwell, a fellow East Anglian. Indeed it seems likely that he knew Cromwell personally, for the latter had written a letter of recommendation for Fromanteel's Freedom of the City of London in 1656—if one can call the written command of the head of state a 'recommendation'. It was following this January 1656 sponsorship that the Royalist Clockmakers' Company administration unleashed a torrent of oppression, blackmail, and persecution against Fromanteel and his supporters. Because of his politics there had been no likelihood of his finding any favour in the eyes of Charles I—as David Ramsay had done. After the Restoration in 1660 he likewise had no chance of noble patronage. In fact Edward East, who seems to have been a Catholic, was then appointed Royal Clockmaker by a near-Catholic king.

If, as seems to be the case, Fromanteel was a protégé of Cromwell, then his time to blossom would have been between 1655, when Cromwell supported his freedom application, and 1658, when Cromwell died. By 1660 Royalism was back in fashion and Cromwell's supporters were definitely out. If he was ever going to make his mark in the horological world, then it surely had to be during these three years, when he had everything going for him. What happened? During these three years there took place developments which revolutionised the British clock trade—emanating from Fromanteel. Was this mere coincidence? I am not willing to believe that it was.

It is my opinion—and, to be fair, I should point out that I doubt whether anyone else shares it—that Fromanteel was the victim of ostracism, of a smear campaign, of industrial espionage, of blackmail and of hostile propaganda for the rest of his life, probably because of his strong Cromwellian links. We know, for instance, that he lent money to officers of the Parliamentary army, and we know that at one point his son-in-law, Thomas Loomes, was imprisoned for hiding the King's enemies at his premises known by the sign of the Mermaid in Lothbury. But all that was to come later.

To return to 1656. That is the year in which Huygens claimed to have completed his first clock with the new pendulum control—he published his findings in a book called *Horologium* in September 1658. Huygens' clocks were made in Holland by Salomon Coster, who under Royal licence had sole manufacturing rights.

This story of the Fromanteels and the pendulum has been told many

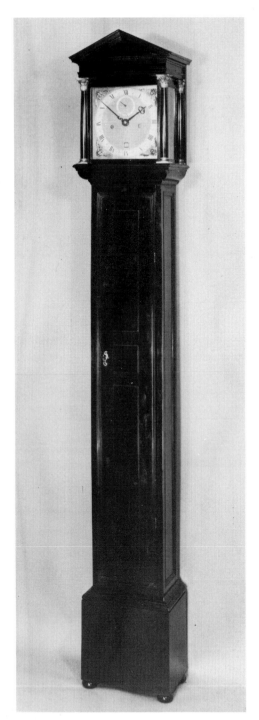

Plate 5. Architectural Fromanteel clock case, *c.* 1670, made of oak veneered with ebony and standing about six feet high. Joseph Clifton of Bull Head Yard, Cheapside, is the only casemaker so far identified as having made cases of this very early type. It is thought that Christopher Wren may have had an influence on the carefully balanced design of these very first British longcases.

times and I would not risk boring you by telling it all over again were it
not for the fact that I do not think it has been told fully. There is much new
insight we can gain by looking at the background surrounding the Fromanteel family at this time.

Coster, the only man in the world with practical knowledge of the new
clock system, opted to share his secret. Who was the *only* British clockmaker
to have access to Coster's exclusive workshop, instruction and technique?
Not Squire Ramsay (as he was called in the Company), not Edward East,
not one of the multitude of French-schooled clockmakers, not one of the
past or present Masters, Wardens or Assistants of the Clockmakers' Company, who were still waging a bitter campaign against Fromanteel and the
rebels. It was Ahasuerus Fromanteel.

Was this coincidence? Did Coster pick Fromanteel's name out of a hat?
Of course not.

It came about through Fromanteel's nineteen-year-old son, John, who
was still at this time apprenticed to Thomas Loomes. John went to work
for Coster for a six-month spell from September 1657 to May 1658. Let's
be clear about this. There was no great shortage of apprentices in Holland,
so it can hardly have been Coster who was searching desperately far afield
to find an apprentice. The motivation must have been from the Fromanteel
side. The known later association between Ahasuerus Fromanteel and
Christian Huygens suggests to me that the whole thing would have been cut
and dried between these two men. They agreed in principle; Coster and
young John Fromanteel did as they were told.

An agreement was made, a 'contract'. It still exists, preserved in the
Municipal Archives in the Hague. In case your seventeenth-century Dutch
is a bit rusty, you can read a full English translation of it in E. L. Edwardes'
The Story of the Pendulum Clock. Among the terms of the contract was one
which provided young John with free beer, but we will not read too much
into that.

The one condition which has had scholars scratching their heads for some
years now is that Coster agreed to show John the remaining 'secret' at the
end of his period of service. A great deal hinges on how literally one takes
the text. Many have felt that this implies the revelation of a *further* secret
apart from that of the pendulum principle, but I think this simply means
that Coster agreed to reveal the pendulum method by the time John's
service had expired. After all, that was the only secret Coster had which the
Fromanteels coveted. When the contract was drawn up Ahasuerus Froman-

teel obviously already knew that Huygens and Coster between them were producing clocks with some secret new regulator. It might be interesting to ask ourselves: how did he know this unless there was contact between him and Huygens? But he cannot have known just what this new regulator was. Otherwise he would not have needed the practical experience which Coster's workshop offered. The Fromanteels wanted the secret of the pendulum technique—any other clockmaking techniques the Fromanteels could have shown to Coster! No, what they wanted was Coster's technique with the new pendulum.

Now, if we assume that there was agreement between the principals, Ahasuerus Fromanteel and Christian Huygens, concerning the John Fromanteel/Coster collaboration—in other words, if we accept that there *was* contact between Huygens and Ahasuerus Fromanteel before 1657, as we know there was later, in the 1660s—then we should ask ourselves why.

Christian Huygens was born into a famous and noble family. He was the son of a learned and wealthy diplomat who had considerable contact with the English Court (a Court where the Royal Clockmaker was also a Groom of the Royal Bedchamber, remember), and he moved in the highest social circles. Yet not only did he overlook the most important and renowned clockmakers in England, who must have been well known to him—men like Ramsay, Groom of the Royal Bedchamber, and East—but he chose in Ahasuerus Fromanteel a man who was *in no way outstanding* as a maker, a man shunned by many for his contrary politics and religion, a man who was a known trouble-maker amongst the respected ranks of the Clockmakers' Company. If we are to believe contemporary records, then the train of events must have run as follows: 'Look here,' Huygens must have said to Coster, when discussing how they might best launch their pendulum into Britain, 'we'll seek out someone who is a clockmaker of no repute and a known trouble-maker, and we'll share our invention with him. That's the best way to go about it.'

Well, inventors are allowed their measure of eccentricity, but such action would imply total insanity. And what about Oliver Cromwell's letter of recommendation? Did Cromwell, too, search out an insignificant maker of clocks, a known rabble-rouser, and put him forward for honours? Was he as eccentric as Huygens?

There must be something very wrong with this argument, for surely Huygens and Cromwell both knew what they were doing. Our knowledge of Fromanteel as a trouble-maker of no particular horological merit comes from the records of the Clockmakers' Company; we are apt to forget that history is written by the victors. When we reflect that what we read is the record as written by a Company where Frenchmen were 'admitted to rule the Freemen', a Company run by the Ramsay-East-Grinkin-Nicasius clan (men who must have been green with envy at Fromanteel's opportunity), a Company who would not put Fromanteel forward for freedom of the City of London until made to do so by Cromwell's personal letter . . . how can we take their word as admissible evidence?

Was it coincidence again that Cromwell selected for preferment the very man who out of all the British clockmakers was to be *the* one to revolutionise the trade within the next couple of years? I just do not believe in that much coincidence.

The Clockmakers' Company tried unsuccessfully to silence Fromanteel. They even punished his associates by disciplining them, as for example when they interrogated the supporters of the Fromanteel petition to the Lord Mayor. The minute books of the Company have it that in April 1657 Joseph Munday admitted that he contributed money to oppose the Company. At the same court Mr Comford (William Comfort) 'did affirme that he did pay to Mr Fromantle and Mr Vernon [Samuel Vernon, another rebel] some money towards the trouble they put the Company unto'. And, of course, Thomas Loomes, Fromanteel's son-in-law, was in constant trouble with the Company administration, who seem to have been over-zealous in their persecution of him.

At this point I ought to explain that the Clockmakers' Company minute books exist in duplicate, the 'rough' books, which were the actual minutes of the meetings, and the 'neat' books, into which the proceedings were later written up more carefully. However, there are occasions where certain events were edited out of the neat books, indicating that a censorship was imposed by the administration—for instance, the incident of 1655, where some of the administrators (Robert Grinkin, Jeremy Gregory and Simon Bartram) had illicitly employed three Frenchmen without consent. This mysteriously failed to be recorded in the neat books.

Even more damning is the fact that the rough books are missing altogether for this very period (1656 to 1673). The story begins to read more and more like present-day political intrigue. The Company had no hall of their own. Their records were kept in a large oak chest at the house of a member; an attempt in 1658 to remove it to another house failed because it was too large to pass through the doorway. Whose house? By another of those strange coincidences it was being moved from the house of Edward East to that of Robert Grinkin, the two ringleaders of the administration. If, that is, we believe in coincidences and the accidental loss of one book in an otherwise immaculate series of records. It is about as convincing as the gaps in the Watergate tapes.

Why did Huygens and Cromwell choose Fromanteel then? What was special about his talents? We don't know, for no work of his survives to display the outstanding abilities he undoubtedly must have possessed. But we'll come back to this in a moment. First let us continue the sequence of events.

In May 1658 young John Fromanteel is presumed to have returned to London, for his term with Coster had ended. In September Christian Huygens published his pendulum secrets in *Horologium*. He did this in order to stake his claim to the invention, because, he complained, others were *already* copying it and claiming the credit for themselves. He cannot have been referring to Fromanteel, for he was given access freely.

In October, Fromanteel published in *Mercurius Politicus*, a Commonwealth newspaper, his now famous advertisement, which I make no excuse for quoting here in full:

There is lately a way found out for making of clocks that go exact and keep equaller time then any now made without this Regulator examined and proved before his Highness the Lord Protector, by such Doctors whose knowledge and learning is without exception and are not subject to alter by change of weather, as others are, and may be made to go a week, or a month, or a year, with once winding up, as well as those that are wound up every day, and keep as well: and is very excellent for all House clocks that go either with Springs or Waights: And also Steeple Clocks that are most subject to differ by change of weather. Made by Ahasuerus Fromanteel, who made the first that were in England: You may have them at his house on the Bankside in Mosses Alley, Southwark, and at the sign of the Maremaid in Loathbury, near Bartholomew lane end, London. There is also by the same Ahasuerus Fromanteel, Engins made in a new way of his own invention for quenching of fire, which have been thoroughly proved, and found to be effective, whereby those that use them, are not deceived in their expectation; for that they are not subject to choak with Mire, and when they are clogged with Dirt, may be presently cleansed without charge, in half a quarter of an hours time, and fit to work again. Neither are they without extreme violence broken, and by reason of their smalness, may be wrought where there is but little room: and some there be so small, that they may be carried up an ordinary stairs in a house, and there used: And are very serviceable for the washing Vermin off the Trees, and Hops, and for the watering of Gardens, and Cloths, and the like.

Plate 6. Lantern clock by Thomas Loomes of London, partner and son-in-law of Ahasuerus Fromanteel, dated 1659.

What is he saying? Well, briefly, 'get your pendulum clocks here', for one thing. But more important he suggests you get them from the man 'who made the first that were in England', not, notice, 'who has just made the first' or 'who will make the first', but who did so some time in the past. How long ago we don't know, but obviously this was long enough ago to have had them 'examined and proved before his Highness the Lord Protector [i.e., Cromwell] by such Doctors whose knowledge and learning is without exception'. Let's not forget that some of these clocks run for a week, a month, a year even: I for one do not believe that Cromwell's scientific advisors would accept proof of a year-clock from a working diagram. There is further the implication in his words that others have since made them, but that he did it first, and of course we know from Huygens himself that even before 1658 others were making them.

Whatever way you look at this advertisement it seems to me to show that pendulum clocks had been produced for some time *before* this. What is so far thought to be the earliest surviving Fromanteel clock is dated 1658, but the authenticity of that date is not accepted by all authorities. How long before, we cannot say. A year? Two years?

Are we to believe that Fromanteel would allow himself to be instructed from scratch in pendulum clock techniques by his nineteen-year-old apprentice son? Obviously Fromanteel must have had some knowledge of the pendulum *before* he sent his son to Coster, which he no doubt did to give the lad *practical* constructional experience.

It would not surprise me if we were able to uncover one day evidence to show that Cromwell's letter of recommendation of 1656 may have been prompted by the fact that his 'Doctors whose knowledge and learning was without exception' had *already* accepted as proven his new pendulum regulator. It looks to me very much that way. Why else would Cromwell sponsor him in opposition to the Clockmakers' Company administration? Where otherwise is the evidence of his claim to fame? Why otherwise did Huygens select him from all others?

And here is an interesting little bit of evidence. In October of 1660 John Evelyn recorded in his diary: 'I went with some of my Relations to Court, to shew them his Majesties Cabinet and Closset of rarities [a room where the Royal curiosities were kept] . . . and amongst the Clocks, one, that shewed the rising and setting of the son in the Zodiaque, the Sunn, represented in a face and raies of Gold, upon an azure skie, observing the diurnal and *annual* motion, rising and setting behind a landscap of hills, very divertisant, the

Work of our famous Fromanteel [my italics].' 'Very divertisant', meaning very entertaining, which no doubt sums up the attitude of courtiers towards the Royal toys. They were great fun, especially if you were a King, for then they were all free.

But notice that this clock showed the *annual motion* (of the sun, one assumes). It may have been a clock which ran for a year, though this is unlikely or the observer would have mentioned the fact. However, if it showed the annual motion of the sun, then it must surely have been a *pendulum* clock, because if it were a balance-wheel type then in the course of a year it would easily have accumulated an error of three or four days, which would have made nonsense of sunsets and sunrises. Unless it were a pendulum clock, which would 'go exact and keep equaller time than any now made', as Fromanteel put it with customary modesty, then the sun could have been rising at suppertime or setting during lunch, according to how far the balance-wheel escapement wandered from the solar schedule. Indeed, the sun feature would have made him the laughing-stock of the court. Does that sound like the Fromanteel we know?

But how did a pendulum clock by Fromanteel get into the Royal Cabinet, for it certainly was not purchased by Charles himself, who in any event had only just come back to England a few months earlier, and had not only reappointed old David Ramsay as Royal Clockmaker, but was shortly to succeed him by Royalist Edward East—Ramsay and East being the two most powerful men in the Clockmakers' Company, which was still persecuting the Fromanteel family. Could it be that this was one of the clocks submitted for testing under Cromwell's administration before 1658, or before 1656 even? It is a fascinating question, but I'm afraid we can only guess at the answer.

What we do know, despite past attempts at concealing the truth and despite a total absence of any sign of recognition or reward from any learned bodies or that supposed patron of the sciences, Charles II, is that Fromanteel revolutionised the clock by introducing the more accurate pendulum regulator to replace the balance-wheel. At the same time he showed great originality of thought in many of the ways in which he adapted Huygens' basic design, an originality shown by no other British clockmaker of the time.

Barely ten years later, Fromanteel's pendulum idea was considerably improved by increasing the short bob pendulum of nine inches or so to a length of 39.13 inches, which had a convenient swing rate of one beat per second. It was achieved by a modification of the verge escapement into the anchor escapement, described fully on page 231 and in figure 14.

It is not known for sure who was the inventor of the anchor escapement, but it has been variously ascribed to Joseph Knibb and to William Clement. Clement, a clockmaker in Southwark until his death in 1704, was apprenticed in 1656 through the Blacksmiths' Company (he was probably then aged about fifteen) to Thomas Chapman and was made a freeman in 1664. An anchor-escapement turret clock made for King's College, Cambridge, bears his name and the date 1671. However, by no means all authorities are satisfied that the clock was built with an anchor escapement originally. Furthermore, it does seem unusual that a clockmaker only six years out of his apprenticeship should have been so successful with this invention to have got the King's College job.

Clement did not join the Clockmakers' Company until 1677—one wonders how he managed to avoid being made to join, if indeed he was working as a master during those seven years. On the other hand, once he did join the Clockmakers' Company (as a turret-clock maker, incidentally) he was instantly given priority of place ahead of men with many years' seniority of membership 'by unanimous consent and approbation and for good reasons and especial esteem'.

William Clement, the clockmaker, has been identified as an anchorsmith who worked at Rotherhithe prior to becoming a clockmaker at Southwark in 1671, the very year of the King's College clock. This identification seems far from certain to me and the whole Clement genealogy needs detailed research, as some facts suggest that there may even have been two clockmakers of this name in succession.

Joseph Knibb (1640–1711) was a famous clock and watch maker at Oxford and London. His claim as maker of the anchor escapement rests on archival statements relating to two clocks in Oxford Colleges. That of St Mary the Virgin is stated in the College accounts to have been converted by Knibb to a pendulum clock in 1670. However, as Knibb is known to have experimented with other kinds of escapements, it cannot be regarded as certain that it *was* the anchor escapement that he applied in 1670. The other clock, that of Wadham College, is attributed to Knibb though it is not known for certain to have been made by him, only *assumed* to be his work because he was the first person to service it. The College accounts, preserved from 1660, make no mention of its purchase, though they do record work performed upon it—which might suggest that the clock was made before 1660. It is recorded that in 1716 extensive work was carried out on that clock, today preserved with anchor escapement in the History of Science Museum, Oxford. Could it be that this was when the clock was converted to anchor escapement? And, if not, then what was the nature of the major repairs or alterations of 1716? We really don't know.

Although Knibb had seven years' standing as a Clockmakers' Company member before Clement joined the Company (1677), Clement was given the senior rank as an Assistant twelve years before Knibb was. In other words, Clement jumped the queue on Knibb by nineteen years into an office that was based purely on seniority of membership. Would the Clockmakers' Company have done this if Knibb had been the inventor of the anchor escapement and Clement a mere graduate from anchorsmith work?

In summary, it does seem as if William Clement was credited with some very special ability by the Clockmakers' Company and he appears to be the favourite contender for the claim as inventor of the anchor escapement.

The pendulum and the anchor escapement—these two basic factors of precision timekeeping were standard by 1680 and set the pattern for the next two hundred years. Britain now had a head start on the rest of the world and very soon became the leading clockmaking country, a position held for a good century or more. With these features the longcase clock, as we know it, was born—the 'King of Clocks'. All other weight-driven British clocks hereafter were no more than derivations from the basic longcase with anchor escapement and long (one-second or thereabout) pendulum.

There was a short phase of experiment with other pendulum lengths, based on the theory that if a long pendulum was more accurate than a short one, then presumably the longer it was the greater would be the precision. A few clocks were made with pendulums as long as was possible; i.e., reaching almost to the ground. Such a pendulum in a longcase clock could hardly exceed about sixty-one inches in length, and would beat about one and a quarter seconds at each swing. It was a phase which died out rapidly; the one-second pendulum was found to be the most convenient length, probably because of its manageable size and the fact that it had a convenient one-second beat.

One development took place as a further improvement in accuracy. This was the invention of the dead-beat escapement, which was a variation of the anchor escapement brought about by redesigning the shape of the teeth and the angles and shape of the anchor pallets. Its aim was to reduce the friction in power transmission, error caused by slight uncontrollability in the recoil and such things in which engineers and mathematicians delight. If you were a scientist timing a vital experiment then I am sure you would have been glad of the extra precision which the dead-beat escapement might have given you over and above that of the normal anchor—if the expansion and contraction caused by temperature changes did not nullify it! The ordinary clock owner neither knew nor cared about this extra accuracy— either then or now.

The dead-beat escapement is said to have been used by Thomas Tompion as early as 1675. However, it was uncommon before the end of the century and is frequently associated with George Graham (1673–1751), by whom it is said to have been perfected about 1715. Nevertheless, it is known that the Fromanteels were making centre-seconds clocks by the first years of the century, and since such clocks must have a dead-beat action, it is quite possible that the Fromanteel family played a part in its development.

Graham is also remembered for his experiments with the materials from which pendulums were made in an attempt to solve the problem of expansion and contraction, which affected the timekeeping of clocks. John Harrison (1693–1776), famous for his work on marine chronometers, also experimented with pendulums to try to solve this problem. These culminated in his famous 'gridiron' pendulum, devised about 1726, in which a combination of steel and brass rods seeks to cancel out the effect of heat and cold.

Although the gridiron pendulum was effective, it was seldom used in normal clockwork. Throughout the eighteenth century high-quality clocks, both London and Provincial, are found in which the pendulum rods are of brass, despite the fact that it was widely known that brass reacts more to temperature changes than does steel. The experiments of Graham and Harrison, therefore, while important in the history of precision clocks such as regulators, had no bearing at all on the manufacture of British clocks in general.

4 The London Longcase

Behold this hand, Observe ye motions trip,
Man's pretious hours, Away like these do slip.
(Verse from dial of a clock by John Ogden of Bowbridge, *c.* 1690.)

—◄◆►—

A Fromanteel example—the specialist parts system—progressions of styles of clocks—ebony, walnut, marquetry, lacquer and mahogany cases

The longcase clock originated about 1658 with the introduction by Fromanteel of the pendulum, initially of course the short (or bob) pendulum with verge escapement. (In plate 4 we see an actual Fromanteel example dating from about 1670.) Fromanteel and his contemporaries were making clocks for the very wealthy, and their products were therefore superbly designed and immaculately executed. They have a simplicity, perhaps born out of a Puritan age, a crispness and clarity seldom equalled again. The workmanship is superb, in no way comparable with early country examples made by clocksmiths, which we shall examine shortly.

On the other hand their customers were paying for the privilege of the very best that money could buy. At this time there were only really two top names: Fromanteel and East. Others were very much lesser lights, basing their work on that of the two top men, and in a sense even East had jumped onto the Fromanteel bandwagon. Having taken for granted that the craftsmanship is of the very highest order, what can we learn about visible clock stylistics from it? We will not get into complexities within the movement, because these very early clocks, while basically of plate-frame construction, do have many variations of layout illustrative to some extent of their prototype nature and we are not likely to see these repeated in later work. What

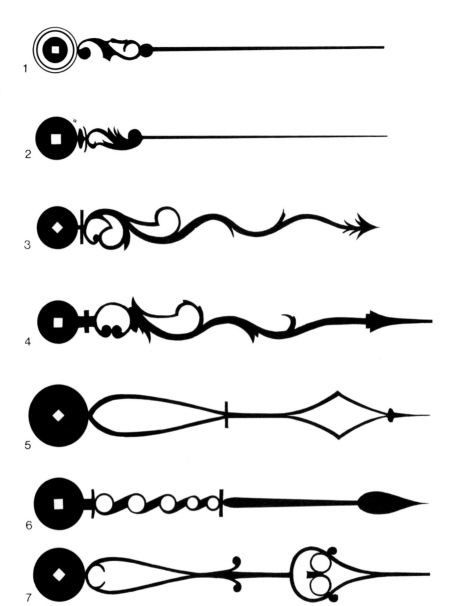

Fig. 7. Some typical longcase-clock minute hands of various periods: all are made of steel except 7 which, although found in steel, is more often to be found in brass. *1* and *2* are patterns found from about 1690 to about 1740; *3* and *4* are patterns from the second half of the eighteenth century; *5*, *6* and *7* are from the period of matching hands, where the hour hand is simply a shorter version of the minute hand. *5* dates from the turn of the century (*c*1790-*c*1810); *6* is an uncommon pattern from about 1810; *7* is a very common pattern from about 1820 to about 1850.

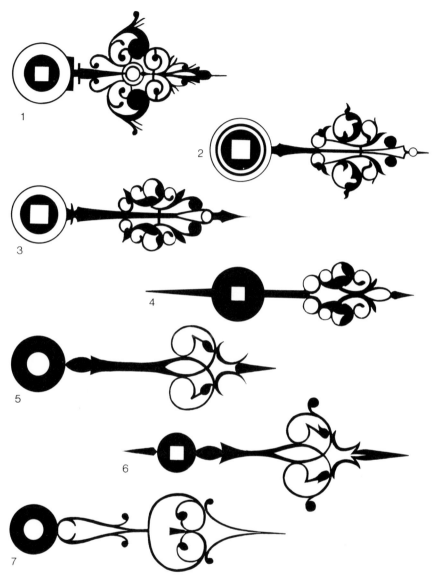

Fig. 8. Some typical longcase-clock hour hands of various periods: all are made of steel except 7 which, although sometimes found in steel, is more commonly found in brass. *1*, *2* and *3* are high-quality hands dating from about 1690 to about 1730; *4* dates from about 1730-40; *5* and *6* from about 1750-80; *7* is a very common pattern found from about 1820 to about 1850. *4* and *6* have a tail, which indicates that they are not strictly hour hands but the hands from single-handed thirty-hour clocks, the tail being used to give extra leverage when setting the time. Each maker naturally varied his designs to suit his own whims, but a great many clock hands are based on these models.

Plate 7. A typical hood of a late eighteenth-century oak-cased clock in a popular Lancashire style. This one in fact is by David Collier of Etchells in Cheshire, but the Lancashire influence extended into neighbouring counties too.

features tell us at a glance that the clock in plate 4 is a very early one?

First the dial is tiny, this one being only 8½ inches square. Dials very soon grew to a normal 10 or 11 inches, but at the start of longcase clockmaking they were very small. The chapter ring is extremely narrow; the minutes are numbered *within* the minute band, and the dial centre is finely matted. On a thirty-hour clock it would probably be engraved, but London clocks were rarely thirty-hour ones and the eight-day examples were almost always matted. It has the very early cherub-head cornerpieces, called spandrels. The maker's signature is along the bottom of the dial plate—it was before long to move to the lower part of the chapter ring itself.

The winding holes are closed off with matted shields behind them (called shutters) indicating that the clock has bolt-and-shutter maintaining power. It was not possible to insert the key to wind it without first bringing the maintaining power into operation by pulling the cord, which simultaneously drew back the shutters. In other words the maker *forced* the owner to use the maintaining-power system, which was a spring that was brought into play to keep the wheels of the time-train going during the time it took to wind the clock, because during winding the weight was not doing its normal job of driving the clock; during winding, therefore, such a longcase became in fact a spring-driven clock.

A maintaining-power spring would usually drive a clock for two or three minutes only, but of course this was ample for its purpose. This device compensates for the loss of the minute or two taken to wind the clock, but this was a trivial time-loss in the space of a week and in any case was easily compensated for by setting the clock to run a few minutes fast. Probably more important was the fact that it avoided possible damage to the teeth of the escape wheel, which on some clocks could rotate in reverse during winding. On later dead-beat escapements it was much more important to have maintaining-power, for this very reason. It is probable that maintaining-power was another Fromanteel invention.

The simple hands complete the style of the whole piece, every part of which proclaims to all who know the signs that it was made in or about 1670, and could not possibly have been made twenty years later.

We saw earlier how the apprenticeship system worked in London, but let us now consider what it involved for we shall need to know this when evaluating the work of the time. The London-trained man was taught by his master most aspects of the craft—and in seven years (sometimes more) he had ample

Fig. 9. Spandrel patterns: *1*, early London cherub head (*c*1660-*c*1670); *2*, early London cherub head (*c*1670-*c*1690); *3*, later London cherub head (*c*1690-*c*1710, later in provinces); *4*, twin cherubs with crown (*c*1690-*c*1725); *5*, twin cherubs with maces (*c*1695-*c*1730); *6*, male head or mask head (*c*1700-*c*1735); *7*, *8* and *9*, three versions of the female head (*c*1715-*c*1745); *10*, small urn, an uncommon provincial pattern (*c*1725-*c*1740); *11*, two birds with urn (*c*1730-*c*1765); *12*, unusual eagle, a provincial pattern (*c*1740-*c*1760).

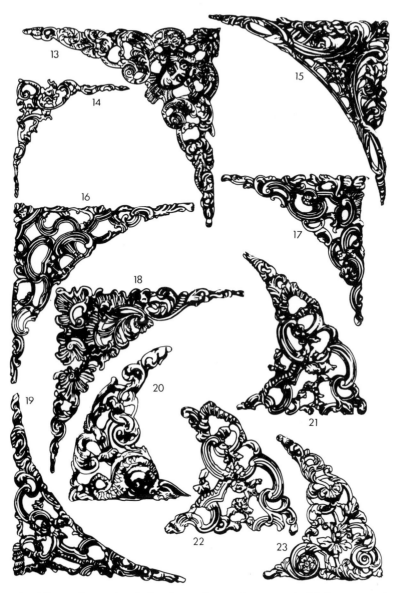

Fig. 9 (contd.). 13, large cherub head, usually northern provincial (c1750–c1775); 14, question mark, usually northern provincial (c1755–c1785); 15, branches (c1755–c1785); 16, castle gateway (c1760–c1785); 17, C-scrolls (c1760–c1785); 18, leaf and scroll (c1760–c1785); 19, string of pearls (c1760–c1785). Arch spandrels: 20, dolphin (c1725–c1765); 21, string of pearls, a partner for no. 19 (c1760–c1785); 22, string of pearls, a partner for no. 19 for shallower arch (c1760–c1785); 23, flowers (c1750).

time to learn. However, while he may have been shown how to execute each function, he would then have passed on to actually performing those more specialised aspects which would form his life's work; this is where theory and practice parted—he had to *know* it all, so that he could judge both the quality and the potentialities of the craft, but he did not have to *do* it all.

The Clockmakers' Company regulations explained that each apprentice should be taught not only clock (or watch) making, but also the making of watch cases in brass and silver, springmaking, and those subsidiary skills such as were involved in making sundials and mathematical instruments and measures. But at the same time the Company sanctioned and regarded as quite distinct specialists within the trade those who made watch 'boxes', engravers, mathematical instrument makers and springmakers.

Most London master clockmakers made their living by buying in parts and assembling them into clocks—while no doubt making their own contributions according to their individual talents. If you were a skilled engraver, you were wasting your talents cutting wheels. Therefore the London trade from quite early times consisted of this fragmented system of part-makers passing clock pieces along the chain of specialisation until a clock came out of the far end. A dozen different craftsmen may have worked at the whole thing, but only one man had his name on the dial—the master, who designed, ordered, caused to be assembled and sold it. This applied even to some degree in the seventeenth century.

Let us take the Fromanteel clock as an instance. Ahasuerus Fromanteel built up a considerable business, and he did not do that single-handed. Each of his sons became a clockmaker, and their offspring either became clockmakers, or, if girls, married them. Each of his daughters married a clockmaker; one married Thomas Loomes, a man already established in his own right, and one married his stepson, Joshua Winnock, who was to produce two more generations of clockmakers. His sister married Andrew Prime, another clockmaker, who in turn produced another two generations in the trade. It is likely that, in the early days at least, most of these people worked in the one business-house trading under the Fromanteel name, a name that was internationally famous.

Much of the trade was controlled in this way by family relationships sometimes extended into business partnerships, and a business-house could thus extend beyond a man's own lifespan, thereby having the opportunity to grow into a large empire. For this reason, the work being the composite output of a whole family group, clocks are often signed by surname only (e.g., Fromanteel—London; Windmills—London), whereas the clock-maker who worked alone, or with a single assistant, would usually put his own personal name on the product. A family may well have had a whole string of specialists within its own confines.

Specialisation was something that the Europeans found hard to under-stand about the British. It may also have been the reason why British clocks and watches in the seventeenth and eighteenth centuries were the envy of the world, excelling in quality those of all other European countries. In 1732 a comment from Leipzig was: 'I must mention that in London different sorts of handicraftsmen work at a clock and those that assemble the pieces and parts that have been manufactured by others are called the actual makers.'

The *London Tradesman* in 1747 summed up the situation with particular reference to watches but of course equally applicable to clockwork:

The Movement-Maker forges his Wheels of Brass to the just Dimensions; sends them to the Cutter, and has them cut at trifling Expence: He has nothing to do when he takes them from the Cutter but to finish them and turn the corners of the Teeth. [See page 244.] The pinions made of steel are drawn at the Mill, so that the Watch-Maker has only to file down the Pivots, and fix them to their proper Wheels.

The Springs are made by a Tradesman who does nothing else, and the Chains by another: These last are frequently made by Women, in the Country about London, and sold to the Watch-Maker by the Dozen for a very small Price. It requires no great Ingenuity to learn to make Watch-Chains, the Instruments made for that Use *renders the Work quite easy, which to the Eye would appear very difficult.*

There are Workmen who make nothing else but the Caps and Studs for Watches, and Silver-Smiths who only make cases, and Workmen who cut the Dial-Plates, or enemel them, which is of late become much the Fashion.

When the Watch-Maker has got home all the Movements of the Watch, and the other different parts of which it consists, he gives the whole to a Finisher, who puts the whole Machine together, having had the Brass-Wheels gilded by the Guilder, and adjusts it to a proper time. The Watch-Maker *puts his name upon the Plate, and is esteemed the Maker, though he has not made in his shop the smallest Wheel belonging to it.* [My italics.]

We must remember that the watch trade was always more specialised than the clock trade and that the situation as described above in the mid eighteenth century was more fragmented than at the end of the seventeenth. Neverthe-less this same principle applied, that the master got the credit for an item which was the work of several men. This explains why, out of the two

Plate 8. Eight-day clock, *c.* 1690, by Henry Elliott. By this time dials had increased to eleven inches square and the much larger expanse was filled in by engraved decorations of various kinds, giving a much 'busier' overall appearance. Ringed winding holes are also a feature of this period.

thousand or so clock and watch makers who worked in London during the seventeenth century, over half of them have no known product to their names—mostly because they worked anonymously either as part-makers in their own right, or as journeymen assistants under a master clockmaker.

For an example of the style of twenty years later we have a dial by Henry Elliott, who began working when he was admitted into the Clockmakers' Company in 1688 and is last heard of in 1697, though he may well have lived longer. We date this clock about 1695, maybe 1690. A lot of changes have taken place since Fromanteel made the previous example. In the 1670s the anchor escapement superseded the old verge type, and the long, one-second pendulum needed a considerably wider case to allow its swing. A tiny dial would have looked inappropriate within a wide hood, and so the dial has increased in size to eleven inches (some were ten). Elliott has used the new style of larger cherub-head spandrel, his chapter ring is wider, and the minute numbering has moved *outside* the minute band. The winding holes are 'ringed', a decorative treatment probably originating in a desire to conceal any scratches caused by careless insertion of the key. This is matched by a ringed seconds centre. The hands are much more elaborate. Decorative engraving around the date-box and here and there around the dial centre is still on a matted background and very different in style from the all-over engraved decoration which a thirty-hour might have against an *un*-matted background. A little engraved decoration between each spandrel pushed the maker's signature up on to the chapter ring. The half-hour markers are more elaborate. The much fussier and more decorative style tells us we have left puritan simplicity way behind. A lot of this decoration, of course, appeared simply to fill up what would have been otherwise much larger blank areas, now that dials are much larger.

This is still a fine clock, beautifully made. It is interesting to compare it with the Fromanteel clock, when the two styles are seen to be in strong contrast. Comparison with the William Tipling clock is also interesting (plate 37).

Our next clock in sequence is by William Smith and is shown in plate 9. Unfortunately we have a choice of several William Smiths and we cannot determine which of them made this clock. The most immediate difference from Elliott's clock is that the dial has acquired a semi-circular top section called an arch. This came into fashion about 1710, and thereafter in London square dials were very much in the minority (not so in the provinces, however). Here the arch is used to carry strike/silent work, which became a very common feature of London clocks. This clock has in many ways become simpler than the Elliott, less elaborate, less fussy, mostly on account of the fact that standards were being lowered to keep the prices down, a factor which had a very great influence on clockmaking over the next century and a half. Of course clocks of especially high standard could be made when the occasion called for it, but the general output was not of such high quality.

Smith has used the older type of spandrels here, a bit outmoded perhaps.

Plate 9. Early arched dial of *c.* 1710 by William Smith, the arch being used to carry strike/silent work, as it often was. This clock can be seen to have bolt-and-shutter maintaining power—unusual as late as this. The square dial was rarely used on London work from now on.

The arrival of the arch brought with it the upright arch spandrel, this particular pattern of dolphins being a very popular one over a long period. The minute numbers are larger than before. The winding-hole ringing has gone, the hands are somewhat simplified. This clock is unusual for its period in having bolt-and-shutter maintaining power, in this case operated by a little lever at the bottom right-hand side of the dial. Of course you would not expect bolt-and-shutter power on a provincial clock—if we exclude the Knibbs of Oxford, because they were not strictly provincial.

The nameplate became a common manner of signing clocks. It left the field wide open for as much or as little buying-in of parts from other makers as the seller wished. For all we know Smith may have bought the entire clock and simply put his own nameplate on the dial. The same applies to the next three examples we illustrate. I am not suggesting that this was the case with these actual clocks—only someone familiar with several clocks by each of these makers could tell us that for sure—but nevertheless I am suggesting that this was the reason for the nameplate method of signing.

John Dorrill completed his apprenticeship in 1732. The clock by him in plate 10 was probably made about 1740. It shows a progression in style from the Smith clock, though not a great deal has changed. The inner band inside the chapter ring showing half- and quarter-hour markers has gone, the half-hour markers between the numbers have also gone. The plain matted centre and plain calendar box illustrate this simpler style, which is typical of London clocks. The spandrel pattern has moved on with the years, but the hands are not much changed. An unusual feature is that the arch here carries a moon dial, which is fairly common on provincial work but unusual on a London clock. Even more unusual is its tidal dial, being the Roman numerals inside the Arabic lunar ones, both dials being read from the same overhead pointer. The engraving around the arch top and on the two 'humps' give it a little character.

Nothing much is known about the maker of the next clock, Peter Vitu, though his name does not sound English. The date 1744 is engraved inside this one, and it seems reasonably safe to take that as the date of manufacture. This clock has the 'four seasons' spandrels, which were quite common on provincial work but are most unusual on a London clock. (I am satisfied that they are original, or I would not use it as an example). Otherwise this clock is typical of ordinary mid-century work. It is an honest and straight-forward clock but in no way outstanding.

Plate 12 shows a longcase clock of the latter part of the century by Charles Absolon. This bears its date on the dial (1789), which in itself is an uncommon feature. It is interesting in illustrating the fact that in London the traditional brass composite dial lingered, whereas in the provinces by this date it had very largely been replaced by the japanned dial. The steel hands are made as a pair, though they do not match exactly as later hands usually do. By this

Plate 10. Arched dial clock of *c.* 1740 by John Dorrill, with moonwork in the arch, an unusual feature for a London clock. Here the fifteenth lunar day is showing. The Roman figures around the moon indicate tidal times, also very unusual on a London clock. High tide here is shown as at one thirty. A switch by the fifteen-minute numeral gives a strike/silent option.

Plate 11. A London dial of the middle eighteenth century, typical in most respects. The Four Season pattern of spandrel, however, is unusual on London work. Peter Vitu is thought to have made this clock in 1744, a date engraved within the movement. Clocks of this time have a plainer appearance than formerly.

Plate 12. Charles Absolon, the maker of this clock, engraved it with the year of manufacture, 1789. This is a most unusual practice on London clocks. The dial centre has now been left as plain brass without the matted surface it would have had in an earlier period.

time we have reached the plain centre, neither matted nor engraved. Spandrels are of a late foliage pattern which is rather pleasing and well-finished.

The final illustration of the London range shows a clock of about 1820 by Peter Grimalde, a man best known for his chronometers. It has a plain japanned dial, quite different from the provincial japanned dial of the period, and the austere look of a regulator, but is a straightforward striking longcase clock, what is sometimes called a semi-regulator. The dialmaker is unknown and instead of a falseplate fitting (see page 237) this has a full-size iron subdial fitting very neatly behind the japanned 'face' by means of pillars and clips.

Plate 13. Mahogany-cased eight-day clock of *c.* 1820 by Peter Grimalde of London. The dial has an undecorated japanned surface for clear legibility. The case is of the classic London pattern of this period, very different in character from a provincial one, although certain Scottish clocks do have this somewhat austere semi-regular look.

This is presumably the London answer to the Birmingham falseplate. The dial is reduced to absolute simplicity, fulfilling its functions and devoid of any decoration. The hands are matching steel pattern. The stress here is obviously on performance and not appearance, the same principle as a regulator, and hence the term 'semi-regulator' so often applied to this type, though without real justification.

The foregoing examples illustrate how London styles progressed from simplicity through elaborateness and back to simplicity. Quality of finish fell off very rapidly after about 1730, which is why the older books give the impression that later clocks are of little interest. In the provinces, on the other hand, the quality remained high quite often into the 1770s. For most periods the London style is very different from most provincial work of similar age, the only real exception being in those early provincial makers who were trained in London. It was of course in bracket clocks that the majority of London makers specialised after the first quarter of the eighteenth century. Bracket clocks were a common London product, rare elsewhere, indeed very rare elsewhere until the nineteenth century. Almost the reverse was true of the longcase clock, which, while not exactly rare in London, was not produced there in large quantities after about 1750.

Let us now turn to the casework of the type of London clock we have just examined. We illustrated in plate 5 the case of the Fromanteel clock. It is made of oak, veneered with ebony, and stands just over six feet high. It is sometimes said, I don't know on what authority, that clocks of this Fromanteel type in the later seventeenth century virtually used up the world supplies of ebony then available. Hence sometimes pear-wood was stained black and used as an alternative, then said to be 'ebonised'.

This case is plain, sombre and dignified. Its beauty must be essentially in either its ebony finish with fine brass mounts to the hood, or in its pencil-slim architectural shape, or both. In a plain clock of this nature it was very important to achieve a graceful design. It is most interesting to compare

Plate 14. (*opposite left*) Month clock, c. 1690, by John Norcott of London. The book-matched walnut-veneered case standing six feet nine inches is typical of this period. Notice the typical barley-sugar twist pillars, the convex moulding below the hood, and the half-round cross-grained beading around the door.

Plate 15. (*opposite right*) Marquetry clock, c. 1695, by John Barnett of London. The outline and proportions of this case are very similar to those of the clock in plate 14. This case is in very clean condition—unlike many marquetry cases, as they are prone to damage owing to the fragile nature of the inlay work.

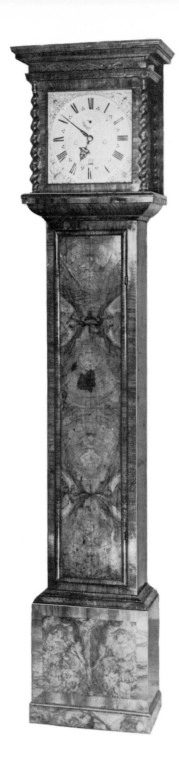

it with its provincial counterpart in plate 74. The main difference is that the Fromanteel case looks much taller, yet it is almost exactly the same height. The reason is that the John Greenbanck case had to accommodate the wider swing of the long pendulum, hence the trunk had to be wider. Some of the later London long-pendulum cases in ebony did have more the proportions of the Greenbanck case, but these early Fromanteels, and clocks by other makers of the time such as East, could attain the unsurpassed grace of very slim cases.

By a rare stroke of good fortune we know who made at least some of Fromanteel's cases for, when one was being restored, a tradesman's token was found where it had been concealed almost three centuries before in a purpose-made cavity within the base. The wording on this token reads:

IOSEPH CLIFTON—HIS HALF PENNY   I.C. 1663.
BVLL HEAD YARD, CHEPSIDE

While this particular case is known as the Clifton case, experts recognise the same maker's workmanship in some of the other early ebonised cases. Yet nothing was known about Joseph Clifton, the very first British clock casemaker, except the brief details he had deliberately left to posterity on his trade token—and had he not done so, we should not have known even his name. Perhaps he did this to record the fact that for the first time ever the clockmaker had turned to a worker in wood for that most important task of making the container and display case—for Clifton must have been aware of the significance of this event. The design of the cases must surely have been stipulated by the clockmakers.

Recently I discovered that Joseph Clifton of St Mary le Bowe Parish was married to Susan Tanfield in October 1658—by amazing coincidence, the very month and year of Fromanteel's famous advertisement. At least three children were born to the couple up to 1665, although how long they remained in Bull Head Yard after that is not known.

The London walnut case is typified by the example in plate 14 housing a month clock by John Norcott, c. 1685. This stands six feet nine inches high and has the typically slender shape of the period, although it is not nearly so slim as the Fromanteel ebony cases. By this time, the wider swing of the long pendulum with anchor escapement had dictated a wider case to allow clearance.

The door and base panel are both of bookmatched veneers, giving a

Fig. 10. The terminology of brass dials. The features indicated may be met with on brass dials over widely varying periods. *1*, moon dial; *2*, engraved corner decoration; *3*, dotted minutes; *4*, engraved dial centre; *5*, leaf-shaped winding arbor; *6*, curved date aperture; *7*, seconds dial; *8*, chapter ring; *9*, dial plate; *10*, cup and ring turnings; *11*, herring-bone engraving, sometimes called 'wheatear' engraving; *12*, square date-box; *13*, nameplate signature; *14*, matted dial centre; *15*, ringed winding hole; *16*, plain winding arbor; *17*, engraving between spandrels; *18*, half-hour marker; *19*, half-quarter marker; *20*, spandrel; *21*, arch spandrel; *22*, full minute band; *23*, Halifax moon, or halfpenny or penny moon; *24*, arch; *25*, name boss in arch.

mirror-like reflection of the pattern based on a centre line. The convex moulds at the top and bottom of the trunk are typical of the period and this type of slender case usually has a half-round beading surrounding the door. Walnut was usually veneered onto an oak carcase.

A grander extension of the walnut case was the marquetry case, also in walnut, and one such is shown in plate 15, a clock by John Barnett of London. Marquetry is often restricted to panels but here it is of the 'all-over' type. Beware of marquetry onto *mahogany* as this may well be Edwardian, or an eighteenth-century mahogany case 'improved' in Edwardian times.

Marquetry cases do not often survive in good condition, as movement in the carcase tends to cause a 'shake' to run down or across the design. There are many people who do not care for the fussiness of marquetry, sometimes described unkindly as 'wallpapering in wood'. However, they are very highly prized among collectors and good examples of marquetry cases fetch high prices—even, sadly, if they contain mediocre clockwork.

Before long, the extravagances of marquetry burst forth into a new fashion of gaudy exhuberance known as lacquer, oriental lacquer, Chinese lacquer, Japanese lacquer or japan-work—all different terms used to describe the same thing, which is the oriental style of painted case shown in plate 16.

A lacquer case, if in reasonable condition, is a prize item and highly regarded by clock lovers. The great majority are in fact in a pretty shabby state. Two hundred years of our climate has often played havoc with them, crackled the surface like a jigsaw puzzle, faded the colours, and worn off the gilding. Most wooden cases improve with age as wax and loving care add a patina and a warmth of colour to them. Unhappily this is not so with lacquer, which began going off from the day it was made, so that today many lacquer cases are sorry things, and it is not unusual for them to have been stripped down to plain oak again (or sometimes pine).

An early lacquer case had a carcase of pine, though later examples into the 1730–60 period were more commonly of oak. On this base was applied a 'ground' of many coats of white powder/paste/gum, building up the raised portions of the decoration into three-dimensional pictures, which were finished by being picked out in reds and golds against a background which was most commonly black. Next to black the commonest ground colour was green, which is frequently met with in provincial examples of the mid-eighteenth century. Much rarer is a blue ground or a red ground (sometimes brownish rather than bright red), and the rarest is yellow.

Early cases are said to have been sent out to the Far East for lacquering,

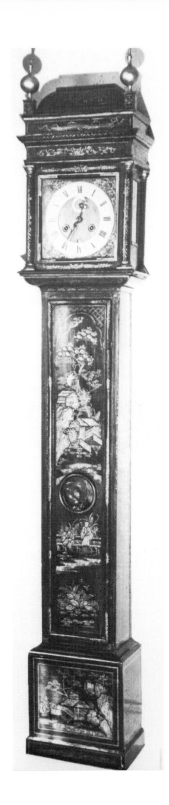

Plate 16. Exceptionally early lacquered case, *c.* 1685, of a rare blue ground colour standing six feet eleven inches, the carcase being of pine. This case, presumably made in London, houses the clock by William Holloway of Stroud shown in plate 36, page 112. The lenticle glass in the trunk door was a common feature in casework of the late seventeenth and early eighteenth centuries.

on a round trip of up to ten years, but I have never seen any actual evidence put forward to substantiate this claim. In some cases just the doors are said to have been sent out. Those who like to believe this may do so, but it seems most unlikely that a London maker could anticipate the fashion of ten years into the future, or place orders for cases ten years ahead of his requirements. Some ascribe the better quality of lacquerwork on early cases to their having been done in the Orient or in Holland, and the somewhat lower quality of post-1730 lacquerwork to inferior English copying.

Plate 16 shows an exceptionally early example, which appears to date from about 1685–90, though most authorities tell us that lacquerwork cases do not begin until about 1700. This case was built (in pine, by the way) with the old lift-up type of hood, as found on the earliest cases, and was later converted to slide forward for convenience, as indeed they almost always were. This can be seen on examination where the tongued backboard used to fit into the grooved backpieces of the hood, and where the former trigger used to hold up the raised hood at the top right-hand side of the backboard. This is a slender example, gracefully proportioned, and standing only six feet eleven inches. It is of the rare blue ground colour. The lenticle glass in the door (cracked) allows the swinging brass pendulum bob to be seen.

Whether or not we quibble as to its being built about 1685 or 1695, it must certainly have been a London case, although this one in fact houses the clock shown in page 112 by William Holloway of Stroud. There would be no local Stroud casemaker able to perform lacquerwork at that time, and it would have been ordered from London for this rather special clock. The convex moulding below the hood is a nice early sign seldom found on a London case after 1700—though occasional provincial throwbacks to this moulding style crop up at very late dates, even in the nineteenth century in Scotland. It can therefore be very misleading to attempt to date a case from this moulding shape alone, as books sometimes imply.

The London case of the later eighteenth century was more or less of a standard pattern, sometimes with a little elaboration. Plate 18 shows the simpler type. It is in solid mahogany, the door and base panel usually richly

Plates 17 and 18. (*opposite*) Typical mahogany London cases of the later eighteenth century. That on the left houses a musical clock, *c*. 1790, by John Wilson of Peterborough; that on the right belongs to an eight-day clock by Richard Kirkland of Glasgow. Both are white dial clocks of the plain white type, which look superficially like one-piece silvered brass dials. On occasion a standard London case was ordered by a provincial maker, as here.

79

figured and sometimes used as veneer on a plainer, solid backing. The hood shape is as shown in the photograph, called by some a bell top and by others a pagoda top. It usually was surmounted by three brass finials—missing in this picture—and it often has a fret in the top centre and the sides. The hood shows a distinct dome beneath the bell top, and has reeded pillars with brass caps and bases. The trunk is long and slim with a door running almost full-length, usually with an arched top to it and a grooved moulding around it. The base has the applied-panel look, though often this is simply an effect produced by using an astragal moulding with cut-out corners onto a solid one-piece panel right across the base-front. The London plinth is usually a double plinth, as here, with shaping on the lower plinth apron. This example has square trunk corners. More commonly there are reeded quarter columns to the trunk, often with brass caps and bases again. On finer examples the reeding of the hood pillars and quarter trunk columns is inlaid with brass

Plate 19. Base of the Peter Grimalde case seen in plate 13, page 71, showing typical London case features found in the late eighteenth and early nineteenth centuries: the width is greater than the height; the astragal beading simulates an applied base panel; and there is a *double* plinth or apron, the lower one shaped for effect.

reeds. On this example the hood pillars have this feature. This same basic case outline was also used in lacquered cases of the period, the lacquerwork being applied to an oak carcase, not mahogany.

Plate 17 shows another example, this one of better quality, having clearly visible quarter trunk columns with inset brass reeding. This case pattern is found from about 1760 to 1800 and therefore can house either a brass or japanned dial. The Absolon clock in plate 12 has a case of this type. So does the clock by Moore of Ipswich in plate 45, and here we come to an interesting point. Plate 18 shows a case which contains a japanned-dial clock by a Glasgow maker; plate 17 houses a fine musical japanned-dial clock by John Wilson of Peterborough. Yet all these are believed to be in their original cases, which demonstrates that a maker in Ipswich, Glasgow or Peterborough, or anywhere else for that matter, could buy in a standard London late-eighteenth-century case. William Martin of Glasgow advertised in 1739 in the *Caledonian Mercury* various clocks 'with the best London cases at the lowest rates'. A good provincial clock, then, *can* have a London case and still be right.

A close-up of a typical London plinth appears in plate 19. It is in fact the plinth of the case shown in plate 13, housing the clock by Peter Grimalde. This shows the Regency development of the standard London case, this example dating from about 1810. It is still a standard type, as one sees many London clocks of this austere semi-regulator pattern dating from about 1800 to 1830. It really only differs from the late-eighteenth-century version in that it accommodates a circular dial, and hence the hood shape follows more closely that of the dial. The trunk door has lost its step and follows a straightforward arched outline. It is no more than a simplification of the later-eighteenth-century type, modified slightly to take the new dial shape.

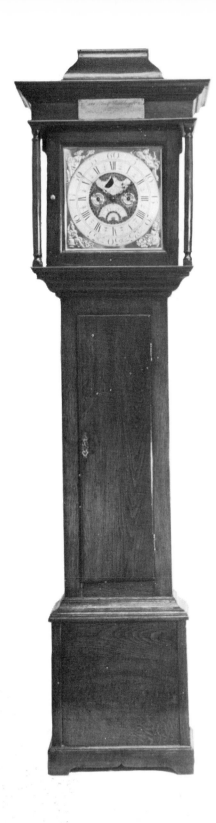

Plate 20. Original oak case made in
1741 for the Thomas Lister musical
clock in plate 31.

5 Clocksmiths and their Work

Here lyeth Thomas Peirce, whom no man taught,
Yet he iron, brass, and silver wrought;
He jacks, and clocks, and watches (with art) made
And mended too, when others' work did fade.
Of Berkeley five times Mayor this artist was,
And yet this Mayor, this artist, was but grass
When his own watch was down on the last day.
He that made watches had not made a key
To wind it up; but useless it must lie,
Until he rise again no more to die.

(Epitaph of Thomas Peirce of Berkeley, Gloucester,
died 25 February 1665 aged 77.)

The two origins of provincial work—clocksmiths—self-sufficiency—a few early examples of their work—economic factors—the workshop of Thomas Power—wheelcutters and other techniques—stakes, wimbles and lares—progression of eighteenth-century styles with examples—a unique thirty-hour musical clock—imitation eight-days

Provincial clockmaking began in two distinctly separate ways. London-trained men sometimes moved to the provinces to retire, to escape religious or political prosecution, to find new markets, to found new empires in virgin territory, or perhaps simply to cultivate their own gardens away from city life. Frequently they were originally 'country boys' who were going home. Whether they were famed masters of the craft seeking a rural haven, or unknown and newly-qualified young men hopefully unleashing their enthusiasms on the provinces, where a tempting nine-tenths of the country's population offered a vast potential market, these London men had one thing in common, namely that they took with them the finest techniques of the trade. Provincial work by such men emerged instantly at the moment of their arrival as a fully-fledged craft, whereas local metalworkers, who developed into self-taught clockmakers—men who were blacksmiths, locksmiths, church bell and church clock makers—developed their own sometimes rustic versions of the trade, often with much cruder techniques producing much cruder work.

The two categories, the London-trained and the self-taught, developed side by side in the provinces. The former would usually cater for the luxury market of eight-day longcase and even spring clocks. They had access to the London casemakers and could offer a marquetry or walnut case or a sophisticated clock of a month's or even a year's duration, or a finer London-school lantern clock. The self-taught provincial makers would usually cater for the cheaper end of the market, mostly with thirty-hour longcase clocks or simple lantern clocks. They had not the same contacts with the London suppliers and their work is frequently of great crudity. The fact that they often cast their own brass, did their own engraving and other such tasks, frequently bought-in by the London school, may endear them more to our hearts but does not bring their work up to the same level of 'quality' as that of the London-trained.

The background of the London man was discussed earlier and was vastly different from that of the local rural blacksmith-cum-clockmaker. The latter had to pick up his own knowledge as he went on, like Tom Peirce, 'whom no man taught', and he carried out a great many functions himself, which the Londoner farmed out. Some of them did everything themselves, even to casting their own brass plates and spandrels, which is why these rustic clocks sometimes have lead spandrels or Cornish tin ones. The country maker cut down on cost wherever he could and used the most readily-available materials. Even the women and children of the house helped with such jobs as chainmaking, though few, I suspect, went to the extreme lengths of the Powley family of clockmakers of Asby in Westmorland, to whom a local mining surveyor referred in 1755 in a survey report: 'in this parish is a coper [copper] mine in which a Clock Smith digs all his coper he uses, having smelted it himself: it [having] so fine a colour, he makes wach cases and sells 'em for pinchbeck. He is all has overworked [i.e., is always overworked]; being in a remote place, 'tis scarce known. . . .'

These country men were often known as 'clocksmiths', a hybrid term aptly describing their trade as half-way between clockmaker and blacksmith—

not that this implies that some of them were not capable of making superb clocks. A clocksmith of course wanted copper for making his brass, though in this instance the Powleys made it into watch cases, which they were able to pass off for Pinchbeck metal on account of its rich colour. One clocksmith, Henry Tyson of Egremont, amused himself by making wooden clocks (as others sometimes did too), but his obituary of 1836 records: 'Encouraged by his successful experiment he next attempted the construction of one, the wheels of which were penny pieces: in this he also succeeded and so well did it keep time that it was used by him in after years as a regulator'.

The early clocksmith aimed to be as self-sufficient as possible, partly because he was in a more remote place and had not the ready access to town suppliers, partly because he was motivated by a desire to keep the cost of his product as low as possible in order to reach more local customers. In many country clockmaking families one finds the transition through the generations from the father as blacksmith to the son as clocksmith to the grandson as clockmaker. The London apprenticeship often cut out one generation where for example a blacksmith sent his son off to learn the clockmaking trade and saw him return as a fully-fledged Londoner.

The fact that the clocksmith may have done most of, or even all of, his own work may arouse in us a greater respect for him than for the London-trained man. However, if we compare their work, that of the Londoner will be seen to be far finer in concept and in quality during this early period, the later seventeenth century, when these men were newly established in the provinces. With the next generation, however, we find a gradual levelling-off process has begun. The son of the London-trained father had to limit the scope of his products according to local demand. Conversely, as the son of the clocksmith gradually climbed the ladder of experience and esteem, his customers increasingly came from the higher income groups, who a generation ago would have patronised only the London-trained man. By the third generation capability spoke for itself and the grandsons were on an equal footing.

By 1700 clockmakers were established pretty well everywhere in the land, though in many of the more remote or less populated regions this had only just taken place. In Scotland, for instance, the first (domestic) clockmaker on the scene was Humphrey Mills, who came to Edinburgh from the English provinces about 1660 in the clocksmith tradition and is known to have carried out the blacksmith-type work of turret clocks and to have made (or sold—

see page 31) the less costly lantern type of clock. Next on the scene, however, was Paul Roumieu, a member of a French family which had been working in the London trade in the earliest years of the century. Roumieu was an apprentice-trained and highly-skilled craftsman catering for the upper echelons—he made costly watches and longcase clocks in marquetry cases.

Lots of these local clocksmith families developed during the eighteenth century—the Listers and Lawsons and Ogdens in Yorkshire, the Deacons of Barton in Leicestershire, the Cockeys and Bilbies in Somerset, Edward Webb of Chewstoke, Abel Cottey of Crediton, the Barbers of Winster, the Snows of Padside, the Bellings of Bodmin, the Moores of Ipswich, the Rayments of Bury St Edmunds, the Simpsons of Preston, and many many more. They are all the more interesting because they thrived without this London background and developed a true 'provincial' craft based initially on clocksmithing. And what is more they did it their way, which means they were versatile, they experimented, they had successes and failures, but they were distinctively and enthusiastically alive, willing to have a go!

Better London work was unquestionably superb, magnificent, way above the level of clocksmithing. But if we examine an ordinary eight-day five-pillar London clock of say 1770 by an undistinguished maker—arched dial with strike/silent work, so stereotyped we can picture it without really trying—oh dear, but it can be dull. To my mind there is nothing more boring in clockwork than the mediocrity of such uninspired humdrum work. Where's the inspiration, the vigour, the sparkle? We have to ask these questions because if we are clock lovers then we are not devoted to the subject so that we can praise the mundane. Should we derive excitement from mass production just because it is two hundred years old? And not only do we see London mediocrity praised on all sides, but can you show me a book that even mentions clocksmiths?

So, let us have a look at some early provincial work. Here in plate 21 is a thirty-hour example by Jonas Barber, the very first maker to work in Westmorland, and this is one of his earliest clocks. Notice that it carries no place-name.

One frequently finds the place-name omitted on early country clocksmith work. Often it can be because he worked at some tiny hamlet (as with Barber), the name of which would scarcely be recognised twenty miles away. Another reason, however, was that such a maker would often take his clocks to sell at a local market when times were quiet—hence he did not want to be pinned down by a name on the dial that was different from the market he was

Plate 21. Thirty-hour clock, *c.* 1715, by clocksmith Jonas Barber, the first clockmaker to work in Westmorland. The tiny nine-inch dial is decorated with cup-and-ring turnings, a primitive feature not uncommon in the North-West at this time and probably done because it was easier than true engraving work.

selling in. Some makers almost looked upon it as having a 'branch' in one or two market towns, and they evidently even took orders and signed clocks with the name of the market town rather than their true home or place of work. This was a habit found in the nineteenth century and was particularly common in Wales, in Suffolk and occasionally in parts of Yorkshire, and no doubt in other parts. It is not unusual to come across a Welsh maker, known to have lived in a certain town, who signed clocks with the name of half-a-dozen other towns nearby, yet who never lived anywhere but in the one place all his life. In 1715, for example, John Sanderson of Wigton, Cumberland, was fined by the Edinburgh Hammermen's Guild as a non-member for having taken two clocks there to sell. This is an indication of the lengths to which some early rural workers had to go to eke out a living.

Barber took the simpler course of leaving off the place-name—at least he did this early in his career. He was born in 1688 at Skipton in Yorkshire, was at Ulverstone in 1707, and married in 1717 at Windermere. He worked initially at Bowland Bridge and then from 1727 at Winster. He lived and died a clocksmith.

The clock shown in plate 21 dates from about 1710–20. It has a tiny nine-inch square dial and a typical single-handed chapter ring with simple half-hour markers of the joined-arrowhead type and of course quarter-hour divisions. The twin-cherub spandrels are of the pattern most often found in early eighteenth-century provincial clocks. The single hand is apparently original. An unusual feature of the dial is that the centre is neither engraved nor matted but has cup-and-ring turnings, which I always associate with the Lake District where several makers used them, although it is not impossible that they occur elsewhere too. One sometimes finds this cup-and-ring turning used as dial corner decoration instead of spandrels (see plate 23).

The reason for the use of cup-and-ring turning instead of engraving and instead of spandrels was probably that it cost less. Barber, newly arrived in an area which had never before provided a clocksmith with a living, was trying to sell clocks—relatively expensive luxuries—to country people who had always managed without them. In the case of the spandrels, cup-and-ring turning saved both time and brass. If he could engrave—and if the chapter ring on this clock is his work, he was not very good at it—then cup-and-ring turning was still cheaper and easier either than hiring a professional engraver (if he had access to one) or attempting to engrave tulip centres himself.

The dial of this clock also suggests that Barber was trying to keep his prices as low as possible. It is very thin and weighs about three pounds, while a London dial of the same period would have weighed twice that. At the prices of the time, this is a saving of brass worth 2s 6d or about two days' wages, quite apart from the cheaper workmanship. This also explains the relative smallness of the dial, which is nine inches square compared to the normal London dial of eleven inches square.

Barber's movement is a plated one but of his own unusual layout and with four steel latches to hold in place the four pillars instead of the normal taper-pin method. The pillars themselves exhibit an interesting feature occasionally seen on early provincial work. The top two are of brass, turned, with the customary centre knops, but the lower two are of round steel rod. Some clocks have them of square steel rod (the Fromanteel clocks sometimes did, see also the John Greenbanck clock in plate 22). Of course on birdcage movements the upright corner posts are often of square steel rod. The supporter for the pendulum spring is simply a square steel rod slit at the end to admit the suspension spring. The dial pillars, too, are of round steel rod, where a London maker would have used brass. Brass could be formed into any shape by casting, while steel had to be forged, filed, cut or turned and was much less easily shaped, but steel was very much cheaper than brass, costing then only a penny per pound weight against 10d per pound for brass. Hence the clocksmiths were willing and eminently able to spend that extra time on the steelwork in order to reduce the cost of materials. Those four latches, for instance, would have been much more time-consuming to make in steel than in brass, which was the material London makers used for them. As for the reason why Barber (and Greenbanck) and others bothered to produce the top two pillars in brass and the lower two in steel rather than make all four of steel, I suspect that they did it because the top two pillars show and the lower two don't. They demonstrated their capability to produce finely-finned brass pillar turnings by using them where they showed, but for the less visible lower two economy was more important.

Occasionally one finds a clock with a pewter dial or perhaps just a pewter chapter ring. Of course, the silvered brass dials of a few clocks have been wrongly described as pewter by those unfamiliar with silvering, but there are occasional pewter examples. Somehow pewter sounds like a more costly affair, but in fact old records show that pewter was about twenty per cent *cheaper* than brass. So once more the reason was economy. And of course pewter had the advantage that it was naturally and permanently 'silvered' in appearance, thereby removing the need for treatment with silver chloride paste. It is surprising that pewter dials were not more commonly used.

Plate 22 shows a most interesting early thirty-hour plate-framed longcase clock signed 'Jno. Greenbanck Fecit'. This maker is totally unknown, but the clock was probably made about 1690. Notice the bold half-hour marker, boldly all-over-engraved floral centre with the early tulip motif, charmingly primitive and probably indicating that he did it himself, and the original single hand. This one has the London-type cherub-head spandrels. The movement has upper pillars beautifully turned and finned in brass and lower pillars of square steel rod, which was also used for the dial pillars. One finds this combination occasionally on early North-Country work, because Southern clocks usually had birdcage movements rather than plated ones. I imagine John Greenbanck was a northerner.

Notice the square engraved datebox above the VI. It is not cut through, simply engraved on the dial as a blank. It was perhaps done to give the

Plate 22. Very rare early clocksmith work by John Greenbanck, *c.* 1690, with bold primitive engraving based on the tulip motif. The date-box above the VI is simply engraved into the design instead of being pierced—perhaps for cheapness.

illusion of a calendar feature without the work of actually making it; or it may have been that the dial was already engraved before the customer placed his order, and as he did not want a calendar, Greenbanck did not bother to cut it through.

Plate 23 shows a very crude clocksmith thirty-hour signed 'John Ismay— Oulton Fecit' probably dating from about 1720. Oulton is near Wigton, Cumberland. Nothing is known about the maker, but a man of this name died nearby in 1724 and it may have been him. The movement is unusual for North-country work in being a lantern-type one with turned brass posts (see plate 24). The very crude cup-and-ring turnings and crudely engraved face below the XII suggest that the maker did this himself (i.e., the dial-

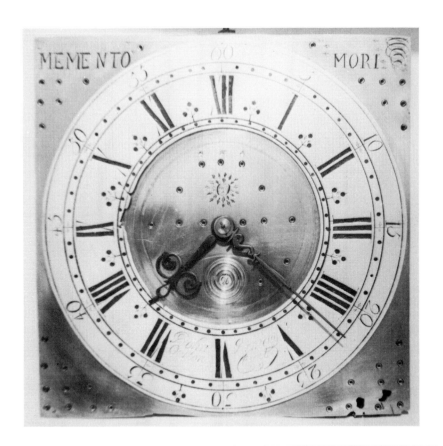

Plate 23. The primitive clocksmith nature of this thirty-hour clock is obvious—flaws in the brass castings, cup-and-ring turnings, crude engraving. It was made by John Ismay of Oulton near Wigton about 1720 and has a lantern movement, which is unusual for this region. It is very crude—but exciting work, for few such survive. Plate 24 shows the posted movement and also the north-country method whereby the dial sheet was cast with gaps in the brass for economy.

Plate 25. Thirty-hour clock by Robert Davis of Burnley, dated 1723, believed to be the earliest surviving clock made in that town. The dial centre displays the popular tulip theme, here very competently engraved. The single hand is original.

plate). The chapter ring engraving is better, though still crude, and was probably done by a specialist engraver. Notice the blow-holes (flaws) in the brass dial-sheet in the lower right-hand corner, with similar casting flaws in the inner chapter ring between the IX and the X. The hands are replacements. This is exciting clocksmith work.

Our next illustration (plate 25) shows a thirty-hour plate-framed longcase signed and dated 'Robert Davis—Burnley Fecit 1723'. Nothing is known about the maker, except that he was the first to work in the town. It has early half-hour markers, all-over-engraved dial with tulip motif once more, nice little chunky original hour hand and spandrels of the less-popular version of the twin-cherub type holding crossed maces and a large crown. I shall never forget that after waiting for weeks for a decision from a local museum when I offered to sell them this clock, I got the reply that it was 'not suitable' for them! I can think of local British museums that will buy exotic French work for many thousands of pounds and will not even *look* at local products of a rare and exciting nature which they could buy for comparatively small change. They will have something to answer for when the country wakes up to recognising its national heritage in clocks. These four clocks ought all to be in museums; instead they are in private hands, the Greenbanck now in Holland. There is something wrong when museums are competing for international prestige objects and ignoring locally-made rarities under their very noses. The unique Thomas Lister musical clock in plate 31 is another that was offered to a local museum and turned down for lack of funds. Such an item will never again come onto the market.

This selection of early North-Country clocks represents clocksmith work at its most interesting—and, surprisingly, only just beginning to be appreciated. I sold three of them, and I'm proud to have had them. Let anyone who thinks these local men did not make their own clocks, and I mean *make* them (for this is a view which was widely held until recently by people who knew the London men did not perform all their own work, and who could not imagine how country makers in little out-of-the-way hamlets could possibly make a living at it), actually examine a Barber, a Greenbanck, an Ismay or a Davis, or any of the many like them, and hang his head in shame.

Before we go any further let's take a privileged look at some eighteenth-century photographs that show us how things really were with a country clockmaker. Photographs? Well, not photographs, but they are almost the same thing: they are extracts from inventories, the lists of goods made when a person died.

Here is a photograph of the shop of Thomas Power of Wellingborough. Old Tom died last week; they buried him last Thursday. His shop is locked up. His widow is grieving. And with the poor man barely cold in his grave, here comes the tax man for his Capital Transfer Tax. With him are other assessors, one with a camera to take a picture of the shop just as it was when Tom finished work at four o'clock last Friday. Let's have a look at it—not at what someone two hundred years later *thinks* it might have been like, but exactly as it was. Let's quote in full:

An inventory of ye goods & chattels of Mr Thomas Power of Wellingborow in Northamptonshire, clockmaker, deceased, taken July ye 7th 1709.

	£ s. d.
Wearing apparrel	3.00.00.
In ye shop	
three clocks & cases	9.00.00.
three other clocks without cases	3.15.00
A spring clock	4.00.00
2 clock cases	15.00
3 new jacks	3.00.00
3 sutes [?] of brass	2.00.00
some work unfinished	1.00.00
working tools	5.00.00
Old lead, brass, iron & other things	10.00
In ye kitchin	
1 wach, 2 tables, 9 chairs, 1 stool, 1 jack	
fire irons & some other things	2.10.00
In ye brewhouse	
a small furnace, 6 tubs & 3 barrels, 5 small kettles,	
2 pottage pots, 6 pewter dishes, 6 plates, trenchers	
& other wooden ware	1.10.00
In ye chamber over ye shop.	
1 feather bed & bedstead, 1 rugge, two blanketts, & a	
set of curtains	2.00.00
2 chests of drawers, 4 chairs, an old box, trunk,	
& other thing [?]	1. 5.00
In ye chamber over ye Kitchin	
1 feather bed & bedstead, 2 blankets, 1 bolster,	
1 old chest, 1 hanging press & trunk, 2 boxes,	
2 old chairs & a looking glass	1.15.00
In ye garrett	
1 wooll bed & bedstead, 2 blankitts & a bolster,	
1 old chest, 1 warming pan & some other old things	1.00.00
12 pair of sheets & other linnen	3.00.00
An old horse	1.10.00
fire wood	5.00
debts due unto ye deceased	7.00.00
sume tot: £	53.15.00

Valued by me ye day & year above written
John Wainwright.
Edward Haller.

Sadly enough, just over two months later his widow Sarah also died and the tax men came again to do another inventory, just in case anything was missed last time. This one was done far more professionally by four men and, for our purpose, is a more interesting and much more detailed survey. Apart from the fact that this time they found a good many other household goods previously overlooked, and having discovered that the 'old horse' actually had some hay as well with the result that its value went up by 60%, we get a clear analysis of the shop contents. The trade items are set out below. The total value this time was assessed at over £83 against £55 last time, which suggests that the assessment was deliberately kept low last time.

One pair of bellowes, 1 anvell, 1 beck iron [?], 2 sledge hamers, 3 hand hamers and a large vice, 3 large screws plates, 1 pair of shires, 4 wimbles, 1 stake, 1 small boyling copper for old silver, 1 grinding stone, new iron and other odd things belonging to the forge	£ 3.12. 6.
One spring clock and cases, 1 week clock unfinished, 1 30 hour clock also unfinished, 2 working vices, 1 half round stake, a turnbench, 1 small stake with plyers, files and other odd things, [5 chests?] of draws, 1 desk, 2 small brass quadrents	8.17. 6.
One vice, 3 pair of compasses, 1 planishing hamer with a benchboard, files and other odd things	11. 0.
One dyal board for a church, 4 clock cases unfinished, 2 saws and other joyners tools	3.10. 0.
Two ordnary clocks, 1 in a head case, 1 unfinished, 1 painted clockcase and 2 old spring cases, 1 large brass quadrent, 2 vices, 1 large stake, 6 steel lares, 2 suits [=sets?] of clockwork unwrought, 1 large jack, 2 small jacks, 3 weatherglass frames, 2 cupboards with files, screw plates, and other odd things	13.13.00
One ingin, 4 brass watches and 1 glass frame, 1 large wooden lare	4. 7. 6.
Two dozen of large new files and 4 dozen of small ones	9.00
Old guns and other lumber	15.00.
One clock and one jack	1.10.00.

This is extremely interesting, but difficult to draw conclusions about values, because we don't know which of the two inventories was exaggerating most, or in which direction. One imagines that items would be undervalued or omitted if possible. We seem, therefore, to be looking at deliberately low valuations and valuations of unfinished goods. Even so, one can see that the spring clock at £4 was a very costly single item. One wonders what he was going to do with 'two old spring [clock] cases'—was he going to refit them with new spring clock movements, break them up to re-use the wood, or had he used their movements or springs again?

We might conclude from the first inventory that Thomas supplied clocks with or without cases, and we may be right. On the other hand the second inventory illustrates plainly that Thomas was one of those unusual clockmakers who also made his own cases, as he had four unfinished ones and the joiner's tools to go with them. We can see that he made mostly longcase types with a very occasional spring clock and an interesting one in 'a head case', which is of course a Hood Clock (head being the term commonly used for hood in eighteenth-century clock terminology). Notice '1 painted clockcase', which would be a pine one painted perhaps kitchen green or teapot brown, illustrating that pine clocks *were* painted originally.

He also made jacks for roasting meat; turret clocks—why else would he have a dial board for a church clock (and clearly not a scrap one)?; quadrants; and presumably barometers, too, as he had three weatherglass frames. He also had four brass watches and, while it is possible he may have made watches, it is unlikely; more probably these were old ones he had taken in part exchange, though they could have been new ones that he had bought in to sell.

We can see that Thomas Power was a very versatile and industrious man. It could be that he employed a journeyman, because one signatory is John Wainwright, who was a clockmaker initially at Wellingborough and after 1751 at Northampton. It is not clear at what date John Wainwright began to work independently, but at this date he may well have been working for Power. It is also possible that Thomas may have employed a carpenter for the casework rather than make it personally.

A glance at some of his equipment will tell us in a little more detail just what he did and how. We see that he had a furnace, bellows and an anvil and grindstone—so he was able to forge his own steel and cast his own brass. He had a quantity of 'new iron' as well as 'old lead, brass, iron and other things'. He would have taken in old clocks and old metals as scrap for re-casting and re-working. He had a 'small boyling copper' for melting down old silver, which also he would have taken in as scrap. Most of these practices are familiar to those accustomed to the ways in which early clocksmiths worked.

The 'ingin' was an engine, that is a wheel-cutting engine, for measuring out and cutting his own wheels and pinions. A wheel-cutter was fitted with a 'dividing-plate' whereby, once the wheel-blank was mounted onto the engine, one selected the number of teeth to be cut and the equal spacing and measuring of the teeth was then performed automatically by the dividing-plate while the cutter made straight-sided slots in the wheel. This is, of course, a very far cry from the hit-and-miss method of doing it by means of a 'true eye', to which someone unfamiliar with the wheel-cutting technique might credit the results. Wheel-cutters were used from quite early in the seventeenth century, although it is not known at what date they began. While Robert Hooke is often said to have invented a wheel-cutting engine about 1670, it is fairly certain that he was not the first to do so. Dividing plates were used even before the seventeenth century began.

The straight-sided teeth left by the wheel-cutter had then to be rounded at the tip by means of a hand file. This was known as 'rounding up' the teeth. With later, more advanced, wheel-cutting engines several wheels of the same size could be cut simultaneously. Later, too, engines which would do the rounding-up as well were perfected.

The 'pair of shires' was, of course, a pair of shears. The 'screwplates' were screw-cutting plates with which he could cut his own screws with whatever threads he wanted.

Among his various hammers was especially mentioned his 'planishing hamer', which had a specially-rounded face to avoid leaving bite-marks on the metal. Planishing was an essential part of the clockmaking process; it involved hammering the flat brass plates or wheel-blanks (straight from the casting-box) in order to harden the metal and to reduce the possibly uneven castings to a more uniform thickness. They were then easier to file clean to a smooth and hardened surface. On some clock plates one can see, for instance, the (hidden) front side of the front-plate left unplanished—i.e. with rough pockmarks of the casting sand still visible—as it was easier for the clockmaker to scribe out his wheel-trains layout on the rough and softer surface. The inside of the front-plate, on the other hand, would usually be planished and polished. With some of the clocksmiths the plates seem to be left almost entirely raw from the casting with little or no attempt at planishing. The hardening was important, as unplanished brass would tend to wear —especially with, for instance, wheel-teeth and pivot-holes, where there would be contact with the opposing steel parts.

The principle was always to try to put brass and steel to meet each other as opposite metals, butting steel to brass and vice versa, since the meeting of steel with steel or brass with brass in moving parts would involve more rapid wear. Steel was, of course, the harder metal and was used for pinions, which have to stand greater pressure than the wheels. However, examination of many old clocks can show that while the steel may be very worn, the brass wheels can look untouched. There are two reasons. Firstly, steel is affected by rust and brass is not, and, secondly, the dirt and grime tends to bed into the softer brass and then act as an abrasive against the steel.

A few items of a specialised nature are lost to us in meaning today—e.g., the 'wimbles' and 'lares'.

The point in examining Thomas Power's inventory is that we can plainly see that there was precious little he could *not* do, and it is often the case that these early makers, especially provincial makers, were very well equipped, much more so than we are apt to realise. This being so they were highly self-sufficient, indeed they had to be, and since they had the basic equipment, this would, as the *London Tradesman* told us earlier, 'render the work quite easy, which to the eye would appear very difficult'.

One interesting piece of equipment comes to mind, an English equivalent of which I cannot locate (though, of course, they would also have had them in England). That is from the inventory of Rudy Stoner, a clockmaker of Lancaster, Pennsylvania, who died in 1769. He left amongst much other tackle 'one machine for making clock chains', valued at only three shillings. It must have been a simple gadget, performing easily what may have seemed difficult. Another interesting item of Stoner's was 'one fuzee engine for clockwork—ten shillings'. This was a device for cutting the grooved cone-shaped fusee. Also mentioned were 'two clock faces—7/6d' and 'one bottle of lacker—2/6d'. The dials were brass ones and obviously not all that costly. The lacquer was for lacquering over his polished and his silvered brass.

This is not to say that clockmakers were not skilful workers, but we must get things into perspective. The real skills came after the machine-work was done. With engraving, for instance, one had much more a handcraft skill than with wheel-cutting, but even then some aspects were done with the aid of machinery. For example, the several circles on the dial plate were executed immaculately, not by running the hand-held engraving tool round the plate in a circle but by holding the graver still and spinning the plate on a lathe or turntable. The free-hand engraving, of course, was a real test of skill.

A clock with a matted centre, as opposed to an engraved centre, was probably easier to execute, especially if you were not too good at engraving. The fine sandpaper finish was produced in order to provide a non-reflective surface as background to the clockhands. It consists of thousands of tiny punch-dots and ideally should be very evenly executed and of uniform depth. The clockmaker did not, however, sit and punch thousands of individual holes or it would have taken him a week and come out resembling a pincushion. He used a matting punch (sometimes called a frosting punch) with a face perhaps three quarters of an inch square carrying a finely-chiselled punch surface. Sometimes even a matting wheel was used to cover large areas more easily.

Those clockmakers who made spring clocks would have a fusee engine. Oddly enough, a fusee engine is not separately itemised amongst Thomas Power's equipment, but it is just possible that he may have bought his spring clocks rather than have made them personally, since bracket clock making was a somewhat more specialised technique and his demand for such costlier items cannot have been great.

Plate 26. Finely-executed eleven-inch dial showing the highest calibre of craftsmanship by clocksmith Samuel Roper of Crewkerne, c. 1735. The engraving style and finish is comparable with contemporary London work. The movement is of the lantern type not uncommon in these southern areas.

Plate 27. A good north-country thirty-hour dial of about 1750 by William Porthouse of Penrith, a prolific and consistently fine maker. The names of the first owners—John and Margaret Parmely—are engraved on the dial; the clock was probably made for their wedding.

Now that we have seen how these clocksmiths carried out some of their work, let us continue with a progression of styles. Plate 26 shows a thirty-hour longcase clock by Sam Roper (1707–1759) of Crewkerne having a posted movement with turned lantern-type pillars. In other words it is virtually a lantern clock with longcase dial. It is a very creditable piece of high-grade clocksmith work and dates from about 1730–40. It has the matted centre typical of many regions in mid century with a little engraving just around the calendar box.

Plate 28. Thirty-hour clocks do not usually have arched dials but this is an exception, made by Richard Stonehouse of Whitby, *c.* 1750. The curved date aperture appeared about this time and for a while became the dominant type. This is a pleasant clock but not outstanding in quality.

In plate 27 we have another thirty-hour clock of superficially similar appearance by William Porthouse of Penrith. This one also carries the names of the original owners and is believed to have been bought for their wedding, which dates the clock at about 1750. It was not uncommon for the original owner(s) to have their names engraved on a clock dial as well as (and sometimes even *instead of*) the maker's, and it seems to have been a favourite habit of Will Porthouse to offer this as a part of his service. This, being a North-Country clock, has a straightforward plate movement.

It is a little unusual for a thirty-hour brass dial clock to be arched, as the arched version was usually reserved for the more costly eight-day type. Plate 28 shows one, however, by Richard Stonehouse of Whitby, made about mid-century. Note the turned roundels where an eight-day clock would have had winding holes and a seconds ring. These are probably to give the appearance at a distance of an eight-day clock. It was not too unusual for North-Country makers to make their thirty-hour clocks look like eight-day ones, some having not only dummy winding holes but even dummy winding squares and seconds dials to further complete the resemblance (for an eight-day clock usually has a seconds dial and a thirty-hour usually does not, unless purposely given one as described above). This deception was probably most common in Lancashire. Often it is impossible to tell whether the clock is a thirty-hour or an eight-day unless one can open the case door or take off the hood. The purpose of this deception can only have been to make it easier to impress the neighbours. Plate 31 shows one with dummy winders.

Plate 29. Thirty-hour clock, c. 1775, by John Lawrence of Lancaster, with calendar pointer positioned, unusually, below the XII. The shields behind the winding holes are reminiscent of maintaining-power shutters, but here they are simply additional trim to camouflage the clock, making it look like a key-wound eight-day. It is, of course, a pull-wind movement like all thirty-hour clocks.

Plate 29 shows a thirty-hour clock by John Lawrence of Lancaster dating from about 1770–80. This, too, has dummy winding holes. The dial below the XII is not a seconds dial, as we might first imagine, but a calendar dial, switched from its usual position above the VI—again done deliberately to enhance the eight-day look. Notice that by now the dial centre style has returned to having engraved scrollwork covering a large portion of the centre, but of course very different in style from the early tulip type of engraving we saw on the John Greenbanck clock fifty years before.

Another type of brass dial appeared about 1775, which was a much simplified form of single-sheet brass dial with no added features such as chapter rings. Everything was engraved on the brass sheet. These are sometimes called one-piece dials. They were not popular everywhere but were found mostly in the south, especially in East Anglia and in the West Country, but this dial style was also popular in Scotland in eight-day work. This example (plate 30) by Daniel Dickerson of Eye dates from about 1780–85.

Plate 30. Single-sheet brass dial of thirty-hour clock, *c.* 1780, by Daniel Dickerson of Eye. The engraving is finely executed and, when new, such a dial would have been silvered for sharp legibility. The movement is of the posted birdcage type, as one would expect in this part of the country.

Plate 31. Magnificently engraved dial of thirty-hour clock by the elder Thomas Lister of Luddenden, near Halifax, with dummy winding squares giving an eight-day appearance. This unique clock plays a tune every fourth hour; it was made in 1741 for, it is believed, the wedding of the clockmaker's brother-in-law. Only three or four musical thirty-hour longcase clocks of British make are known to exist.

As an example of an outstanding thirty-hour provincial clock, plate 31 shows one by the elder Thomas Lister of Halifax, who worked from about 1740 at Luddenden, a hamlet whose only claim to fame is to have had its existence doubted in *A Collector's Dictionary of Clocks* by Alan Lloyd because he could not locate it on the map. Well, it is there. This clock is signed at Luddenden, showing it to be one of his early products before Lister moved to Halifax, but what might initially appear to be a beautiful eight-day is in fact a thirty-hour with dummy winding squares. This is one of those extreme rarities of which barely a handful exist at all—a thirty-hour *musical* clock playing a tune on six bells every fourth hour, at 12, 4 and 8 o'clock. It has a thirty-hour movement with strike on one chain and a separate chain-driven train for the music, and the movement has beautifully shaped baluster pillars and handsomely decorated twin outside countwheels at the back (one for the strike and one for the music).

The case has a brass plaque attached to the hood giving the music, the date of making (1741) and the names of the first owners (Isaac and Mary Holdroyd) so that we know exactly when it was made. Thomas himself had married a Holroyd only four years before and it is thought that this very special clock was made for his brother-in-law's wedding. The dial is a magnificent example of ornate engraving—the elder Lister was probably one of those who *could* do his own engraving. Notice the flourishing leaf engraving on the initial letters of the signature and the magnificently executed herringbone engraving around the centre and around the moon and calendar apertures. The winding squares are shaped into four-leafed stars, although only dummy winders.

Surrounding the whole dialsheet is a semi-circular applied brass beading, a feature more usually associated with Lister's great rival, Thomas Ogden. The whole execution of this clock shows that Lister was not producing thirty-hour clocks for reasons of economy, and it remains a puzzle why makers of this obvious ability did tend to stick to thirty-hour clocks. There is no known example of eight-day work by Thomas Lister senior, though there are many by Thomas Lister junior, whose work is very different, being much inferior in quality despite including a number of very complicated astronomical clocks. One wonders whether there was perhaps some factor in thirty-hour clocks which we have forgotten how to appreciate today— such as perhaps that the daily winding was seen as a part of the pleasure of ownership rather than the bore that we often see it as today. Anyway here is a superb example of clocksmith work at its best.

If we run back through the illustrations they can be seen to elucidate the change in style over the course of the century. The early ones are single-handers, and while this type was still common into the 1760s, by about 1770 the two-hander was beginning to dominate. By the end of the century it was really only in the very traditionally slow-moving areas that the one-hander persisted—regions such as East Anglia, where even japanned dials are sometimes seen in single-handed form still with the old birdcage movement, long after it was superseded elsewhere.

The single-hander shows the quarter-hour divisions, marked off on the double band inside the chapter ring (see plates 21–25). The same inner

Plates 32 and 33 (*opposite*) A glimpse at the superb Lister musical movement reveals exceptionally intricate pillars and the musical barrel with wedges to trip the six numbered hammers onto the nest of bells. The linked twin locking-plates can just be seen. An example of the very best in British clocksmith work.

chapter-ring quarters often showed on two-handers too, where additionally the half-quarters were usually indicated by an asterisk, star, diamond or other device—the Sam Roper clock shows this. Half-quarters were marked at $7\frac{1}{2}$ minutes past and to the hour and at $22\frac{1}{2}$ minutes past and to. The half-quarters gradually fell out of use during the first quarter of the century, as did the inner quarter-hour markers. By 1730–40 the half-quarter markers had usually gone; by 1750 the inner quarters had also been dropped by most makers, although the half-hours were still marked, usually by a fleur-de-lys or other symbol accentuating the half-hour mark on the inner band. The

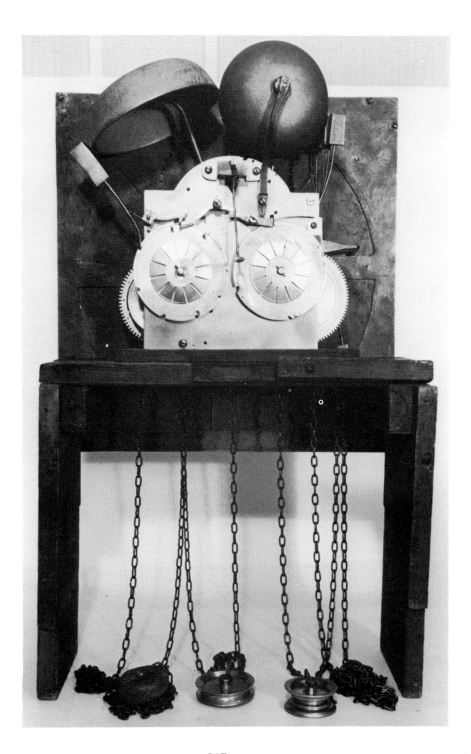

Plate 34. Thirty-hour longcase clock of about 1780 by Thomas Lister junior. The engraving is finely done, although it is believed that he did not do his own engraving. The work, however, is of poor quality when seen alongside that of his father (plate 31, page 104)—for example, the spandrels can be seen to have been left unfinished with the casting 'rag' still present.

Porthouse dial shows this mid-century stage where the quarter-hours and half-quarters have been dropped but the half-hour markers and symbols persist. By the date of the Stonehouse clock these have both gone too and the space between hour and minute numerals is left plain, and was to remain plain thereafter.

The Lawrence clock in plate 29 illustrates the next development in style in that the minutes are now marked by dots instead of the full double band. This begins about 1775 and was probably copied from the dotted minute style of the earliest japanned dials. The clock by Daniel Dickerson of Eye (plate 30) illustrates a variation on the late eighteenth-century theme, the only real difference being that this is a single-sheet type of engraved dial.

The treatment of the dial centre also varies with age. The earliest dials have engraved centres (possibly derived from lantern clocks), reverting usually to a matted (or frosted) centre around mid-century, and then there was a return to an engraved centre by the 1760s, though engraved centres in this later period were of a very different style from the earlier period and were more common in the north than in the south, where some clocks remained matted throughout the later part of the century. The above relates to thirty-hour clocks; and while it applies to some degree to eight-day clocks, these have a stronger tendency to retain the more austere matted centre, especially in the south and virtually always in London.

Another stylistic development can be seen in the means by which the calendar is shown. Simpler thirty-hour clocks tend not to have this feature. On early clocks the calendar usually shows through a square (sometimes circular) aperture immediately above the VI numeral. By mid-century this usually develops into a curved semi-circular opening (sometimes called a lunette, though this term is a little confusing, being also used to refer to a type of moon dial). This can be seen on the Stonehouse example (plate 28). Later in the century the calendar is often indicated by a pointer, as with the Lawrence example, though normally still positioned above the VI.

Another feature sometimes said to be indicative of period is the increasingly wide chapter ring. However, as dials also gradually get larger, from nine or ten inches at the beginning of the century to around twelve or thirteen inches towards the end of it, the increasing chapter ring width is not always obvious, as it stays in proportion to the dial size. Eventually the chapter ring disappears altogether with the single-sheet examples, which were common in certain areas in the last quarter of the century.

Plate 35. (*overleaf*). Very fine mahogany case about eight feet tall housing an eight-day clock by William Tickle of Newcastle on Tyne, *c.* 1770. The case shows considerable 'Chippendale' influence, particularly in the lavish use of magnificently executed blind frets to the hood, and in the 'impost'. Notice the fine key-pattern mouldings to the hood and the arcading below the upper hood mould. The pillars have brass Corinthian caps and bases and are double-reeded with brass inserts. The tea-caddy canopy gives the hood a heavy appearance, which although here balanced by a taller-than-average base, is a characteristic of cases from this region. A superb example of North-country casework preserved in good condition.

6 Provincial
Eight-day Longcase Clocks

A variety of eight-day long clocks & timepieces in mahogany or wainscot cases; timepieces for chapels or gentlemen's kitchens with large or small dials. Clocks & watches lent out by the month or year.

(advertisement of N. MacPherson of Edinburgh, 1783.)

———◄◆►———

Latinisation of names—early examples by William Holloway of Stroud—Tipling of Leeds—Jordan of Chatham—Nicholson of Whitehaven—Lees of Bury—signs of engraved outwork—Parkinson of Lancaster—an Ogden world time dial—Broderick of Kirton—Shaw of Lancaster—Moore of Ipswich—Lane of Bristol

We have already seen the clocksmith side of provincial work. From the later seventeenth century until the mid eighteenth century most provincial clocks are likely to be thirty-hour longcase ones and exciting and interesting examples of clocksmith work. Here and there a lantern clock will crop up, or a hooded clock, or a hook-and-spike birdcage type. Occasionally an eight-day clock will appear, usually by a London-trained or London-influenced maker, the sort of man who would also have made the very occasional bracket clock.

As we get further into the middle years of the eighteenth century, eight-day clocks become more common, both from the descendants of the London-schooled men and from those of the clocksmiths. The two different techniques gradually fused into one. The eight-day clock, however, was always about twice the price of the thirty-hour, and so was always the less common

Plate 36. The ten-inch dial of an exceptionally early provincial eight-day clock, *c.* 1685, by 'William Holloway at Stroud'. Simplicity, even austerity, is the dominant characteristic of such early clocks, the tone being set by the large plain expanse of the finely matted dial centre. It is interesting to compare this dial with that by Fromanteel in plate 4, page 42.

of the two types until the end of the eighteenth century and even after.

Early clocks often had the name of the maker and town Latinised. Some country makers copied what the earliest London masters did when they signed, e.g. 'Johannes Fromanteel Londini fecit'. Fecit means 'made it', Londini means 'at or in London' (not 'of London'). In the provinces makers had a struggle in so far as many a provincial town name could not be declined without a very peculiar result—such as Wigani, Halifaxi, Yorki or Bathi.

Some used the Roman town name, such as 'R. Rontree—Ebor.' meaning 'R. Rowntree in York'. But then many people might fail to recognise the Latin name of the town, and of course the advertising was important. Many therefore compromised by using English prepositions such as 'Thomas Cruttenden *in* York'. Some still tried to give a sophisticated look by using the Latin/French 'de', such as 'Hindley de Wigan', 'Thomas Ogden de Halifax'. Latinisation of names was common in London up to about 1720, in the provinces it appears up to about 1750, though it was not used by every maker.

Our first example shows a maker who stuck to his Anglo-Saxon background. Plate 36 shows a very early example of a provincial eight-day clock. It is exceedingly rare for a variety of reasons, not least being that provincial clocks of about 1680–85 are very rarely met with today. The ten-inch dial makes a most interesting comparison with that by Fromanteel in plate 4. Its small size and austerity, the signature below the chapter ring, the half-hour markers, the centre without any engraving, and the small square date-box are all similar. In some ways however there had been a move towards the Elliott style—chapter ring a little wider, minutes outside the band, larger pattern of corner spandrels, ringed winding-holes and more elaborate hands.

This clock is signed below the chapter ring 'William Holloway at Stroud'. He is known only for lantern clocks dated between 1666 and 1679. The movement originally had bolt (without shutter) maintaining power, now removed. It has five beautifully finned pillars, the centre one latched and the four corner ones pinned outside the *back*plate, an unusual practice. Strike-work is of the *outside* locking-wheel type with the tiny locking wheel placed high up the backplate. Most of these features are indicative not only of very early work, but of very early London work. There is no known London connection with William Holloway, but his work shows distinctly that he was familiar with current London practice while retaining certain individualities in construction that show that this was not simply a clock 'bought-in' from London. This clock is worlds apart from country clock-smith work and outstanding in every way. It is housed in a rare blue lacquer case (shown in plate 16), which would certainly have been specially ordered from London, as there would have been very little local demand for this costly style in Stroud, nor would there have been a local man able to perform such work.

In plate 37 we have an example of an early provincial eight-day clearly

Plate 37. Fine eleven-inch dial of a clock signed on the dialplate 'William Tipling in Leeds fecit', made 1700–1710. The engraving between the spandrels and around the date-box reveals an increasing elaboration, displayed most prominently in the exceptional hands, with a decorative pierced and filed collar around the centre of the hour hand. This is a typical London-schooled dial as executed in the provinces.

from the London school, by William Tipling of Leeds. He is known to have worked there from 1692 till his death in 1712, a fairly short span which helps us date this clock at *c.* 1700–1710. He was almost certainly an apprentice of John Williamson, who himself was a London worker being free in the Clockmakers' Company in 1682 and moving directly to Leeds in 1683. The clock is obviously of high quality. If it were London work it would be good; as provincial work it is exceptionally good and exceptionally early.

This is a documented example of the way the London school reached the provinces. The hands are especially fine, having a large fretted boss to the hour hand. It has inside locking-wheel striking and five finned and pinned pillars.

It is interesting to compare this clock with that by Henry Elliott in plate 8 as they are very similar in style. Tipling uses the slightly old-fashioned (for this date) method of signing at the base of the dialsheet, and his hands are very much better than Elliott's. In fact the Tipling hands are superb—he could probably have given the best London men a tip or two at making hands. The pierced boss on the hour hand is very fine work and is used as an alternative to the engraved hands-centre design on the dialplate, a more normal example of which is seen on the Elliott clock. The Tipling clock might be five years or so earlier than the Elliott, or it might be that his style remained static at the stage of development it had reached when his master left London. In other words the style of a provincial clock can often lag a few years behind London styles, but the suggestion sometimes made that this provincial style-lag amounted to twenty-five years or more just does not stand up to examination. The eleven-inch dial by James Jordan of Chatham (plate 38) dates from about 1715–20. The minute numbers are a little larger, the ringing of the winding holes a little more pronounced, the engraving around the datebox is a little bolder and the spandrel pattern is of a new type. This clock has inside locking-plate striking.

Provincial eight-day work is uncommon until mid-century, except as examples of work by those trained in London, or trained by London-taught masters, and even these are scarce. In plate 39 we see an early eight-day clock by William Nicholson of Whitehaven, made about 1740. It is difficult to be accurate about the date, as nothing is known about the maker. It has obviously moved on from the Tipling/Elliott stage, but in no way resembles the Dorrill/Vitu style. This is not because of differences in period but because henceforth provincial work went its own way, and it would be just as misleading to try to date the Whitehaven clock by comparing it to a London example as vice versa, though this has never stopped some past authorities from trying to do the former, who would never have dreamt of doing the latter. We must forget all about London work and treat provincial clocks on their own merits.

Nicholson's clock retains the ringed winding holes; the half-quarter markers as diamond-shaped motifs; the square date-box with engraving around it; the matted background to the dial centre; and the half-hour and

Plate 38. The eleven-inch dial from a clock of *c.* 1715, signed 'Jams. Jordan Chatham fecit', typical of the first quarter of the eighteenth century. The style has progressed slightly from that of plate 37, page 114. While this is a provincial clock, the London influence is obviously very strong, Chatham being close to London itself.

quarter-hour divisions within the inner chapter-ring band. On provincial work most of these features lingered till about 1745–1750. However in some ways he has progressed—the spandrels pattern, the 10, 20, 30 seconds-dial markings (compared to the earlier 5, 10, 15), the broader chapter ring with wide minute numbers and the hands patterns are all advanced features. It is a good clock, unusual simply by being an eight-day of this age, unusual too in the quality of craftsmanship it exhibits alongside that of London work of the same period.

The winding squares themselves, just visible within the ringed holes, are file-shaped into a four-leaved-clover pattern, just one measure of the trouble and pride he took, which is very much evidenced within the clock movement itself. The movement has repeating work with double levers so that it can be made to repeat from *either the left or right hand side* according to how the

Plate 39. Eleven-inch dial by William Nicholson of Whitehaven, made about 1740. Lozenge-shaped half-quarter markers stand out clearly and the flower-petal shape of the winding squares is a sign of fastidious workmanship.

owner wishes to set up a repeating cord. We would be unlikely to find repeating work in a London longcase of this period, much less repeating work with an either-side option.

The fact that this clock has a square dial is not a feature which helps when dating it. By this time almost all London longcases would have arched dials. In the country at large, arched dials were somewhat exceptional at this early period, perhaps because square dials enabled the total height of the clock to be kept down.

Another eight-day clock from about this same period (*c.* 1740) is shown in plate 40, this one by Jonathan Lees of Bury. It has some features not dissimilar to the Nicholson clock. The most obvious difference is that the matted dial-centre has a deeply engraved design all over it. In the 'matted centre' period (roughly up to 1750 on eight-day work) there was a strong

Plate 40. Eleven-inch dial, *c.* 1740, by Jonathan Lees of Bury. The original hands are of high quality and the engraving is outstandingly good, although perhaps not done by Lees himself. The dial centre, consisting of an all-over engraved design against a matted background, is normally a pointer to north-country work.

variation between North and South. In the North such matted centres often, though not always, had some amount of engraving into the matting, covering sometimes a small area around the calendar box, but more often running away across the whole centre, as with this example. In the South it was more normal for the matted centre to be left without any engraving, or perhaps with a very small area of it around the date-box. The matted *and* engraved centre of the Jonathan Lees clock is very different from the engraved centre designs found later in the century, say after about 1760, which are on a plain (not matted) background.

The Lees clock has many of the same features found on the Nicholson one, but the hands are far more elaborate and beautifully made. This clock has one feature which ought to arouse the suspicions of anyone who is accustomed to looking at clocks, and that is that the winding holes are cut *through* the engraved design and interrupt it. This is a very suspicious sign on any clock, because many a clock which began life as a thirty-hour and was later fitted with an eight-day movement shows this evidence, where someone later cut through the dial to make winding-holes where none previously existed. Such a sign should warn one to look out for other internal signs of a changed movement.

However, this example has the original eight-day movement, so how do we explain the apparent inconsistency between a beautifully engraved dial-centre and the cutting of holes to break into the design? Clearly the holes must have been cut *after* engraving, otherwise the engraver would have worked his design around the holes (as can be seen with the Thomas Shaw clock in plate 44). It may be an indication that Lees could not do his own engraving. If he sent his dialsheets out to an engraver, and if he sent out several at a time, then he would not know in advance which ones were destined for eight-day and which ones for thirty-hour clocks. The bulk of his clocks were most probably thirty-hour ones. On the odd occasion when he was asked for an eight-day one, he would simply cut two winding holes, even if it meant, as here, that he had to cut into the design.

Another feature seems to confirm the view that he could not engrave. His name is engraved on the chapter ring in such a way that it cuts into the numbers. This suggests to me that his name was simply added to an already-engraved chapter ring, such as an engraver might have kept in stock ready for selling when an order came in, just with the naming to be performed as the last act. A man doing the whole job and having taken such care with his chapter ring would have also taken more care to plan the way the name fitted between numbers, which strengthens the suspicion that the clockmaker was *not* his own engraver.

The Lees clock is very fine, with a superbly decorated movement, finned pillars, and repeating work. The Nicholson and Lees clocks illustrate a point, namely that provincial eight-day work of mid-century or earlier is usually of a very high standard of execution, certainly in terms of the movement if not always in terms of an immaculately planned dial.

The clock in plate 41 is signed 'Parkinson—Lancaster' and is probably by William Parkinson, father of a whole family of clockmakers, and made about 1750–1760. Here the matted centre is retained, but the inner chapter ring quarter-hour markers have gone, and the hands are simplified. The spandrels are of a late cherub-head style, quite different from the early London cherub-head. This happens to be an arched dial, more costly than the square type

Plate 41. Twelve-inch arched dial by Parkinson of Lancaster, *c.* 1755. The arch spandrels chosen are rather small for the dial, though original. The wavy 'Dutch' minute band is not uncommon on Northern clocks of this period.

and often housed in a fine mahogany case, as with this one. In this clock the arch serves no purpose but decoration. The maker's name on the chapter ring suggests that his normal output may have been square-dial clocks, and the arch boss, used by many to bear the maker's name, is here simply decorative.

One different feature is that the chapter ring shows an unusual wavy band for minute markings. This is known as a Dutch minute band (some Dutch clocks have this feature) and appears mainly on arched dials of mid-century, frequently when combined with the large cherub-head spandrel, as here. Ringed winding holes here are a late instance. This clock also has repeating work, which in itself is often the sign of a good clock.

Plate 42. The thirteen-inch dial of a very fine clock by the famous Quaker clockmaker, Thomas Ogden of Halifax. This dates from about 1750 and is believed to be the earliest known provincial example of a world time-dial clock. The rotating painted sun indicates by its top pointer when noon is reached in the countries marked above. The floral engraving of the dial centre against a matted background is typical of North-country work of the period.

The clock in plate 42 by Thomas Ogden of Halifax looks superficially similar to the Parkinson one with the exception of the arch area. It was made about 1750. One comes to expect a clock by this maker to have some unusual features and this is no exception. The arched area shows, not a moon dial, as might commonly be found in such a position, but a *sun* dial. It is in fact a world-time dial clock, and a very early example for this type of clock. Quite a number are known of varying degrees of complexity, by (for instance) the younger Thomas Lister of Halifax, Barker of Wigan, and others, but those all date from considerably later in the century, and this Ogden one is the earliest one known to the author. At twelve noon the sun is overhead at the position reading London on the arch. As the day goes on it shows when noon arrives at such places as Jamaica, Cape Breton, Madrid, and many others. This of course was information of an interesting but quite useless nature, and it is difficult to imagine anyone who might have had a special need for such knowledge, other than for the pure fun of it, or perhaps to impress visitors to a business house with overseas connections. It is illus-

Plate 43. Eleven-inch eight-day dial of about 1770 by Thomas Broderick of Kirton (Lincolnshire). The engraved dial centre carries a design (against a plain background) in what we now term the Chinese Chippendale manner.

Plate 44. This twelve-inch arched dial clock made in 1777 by Thomas Shaw of Lancaster is unusual in having a painted landscape set into the arch, whereas a moon dial inset would have been more normal. This is a centre calendar clock, the brass date hand registering the twelfth of the month.

trative of Ogden's skill that he could not only make the necessary calculations but could also construct it. Ogden was a clever man and a first-class workman too. He was a Quaker, and clockmakers of this faith are renowned as makers of sturdy, honest clocks. The same could not be said of the younger Thomas Lister from the same town, who made extremely complicated musical and world-time dials, but who also turned out some very poor thirty-hour work.

Thomas Broderick of Kirton (Lincolnshire) made the square dial eight-day clock in plate 43 about 1760–1770, showing that they were still made in this shape, but not so often by this date. On this example the spandrel pattern has advanced further, the inner chapter ring half-hour and quarter-hour markers have dropped, the hands are still of late eighteenth-century non-matching pattern in blued steel, but the most obvious development is in the dial centre. This has what is termed an 'all-over engraved' pattern, in this instance of Chinese-type buildings and floral sprays in what we might now call Chinese Chippendale taste, although it was done by engravers who had never heard of Chippendale and was simply a reflection of the taste of the time. The engraving is done on a plain surface (compare the

Plate 45. Arched dial clock by Thomas Moore, a famous Ipswich maker, dating from about 1770. The strike/silent feature is common on Southern arched dial clocks, which frequently, as here, have a much plainer appearance than their Northern equivalents.

earlier matted background). Notice that the seconds dial is engraved on the centre with no separate chapter ring. This was normal with this type of dial and less time-consuming. These 'all-over engraved' centres on plain backgrounds were usually silvered over, just as the chapter rings and applied engraved areas were.

The clock in plate 44 was made in 1777 by Thomas Shaw of Lancaster—the date is engraved inside the movement. It shows several features typical of better-class North-Country work at this time. The arched dial in this instance has a painted local scene in the arch (some have moonwork). It has the questionmark type of spandrel often used in the north with a large dial. The all-over-engraved centre in this instance has the numbers one to thirty-one around its rim, showing that the clock has a concentric calendar hand, here indicating the twelfth. This type of calendar was popular in the north but not in the south. It is my feeling that dotted minutes usually indicate work later than 1770.

As a contrast, a southern eight-day clock by the Moores of Ipswich, a well known clockmaking family, is shown in plate 45. This dates from about 1760–1770; it is difficult to be precise because southern styles tended to remain more static than northern ones. A southern clock with a plain (or matted) centre might look like this one if made at any time from 1750 to 1790. The strike/silent feature in the arch is perhaps the most common of all arch devices in the south, while in the north it is somewhat uncommon. In the north arched moonwork was popular on brass dials, whilst in the south it was less so, perhaps with the exception of coastal towns where it might be incorporated with a tidal dial. Our next example shows one of this type.

The clock by Henry Lane of Bristol (plate 46) was made about 1780. Its engraved centre is perhaps not strictly typical. The moon's age is reading the sixteenth in the picture. High-tide time is read along the top row of Roman numbers, and here it is shown as 7.30. Both indications are shown by a pointer on top of the moon face. In the illustration the moon has just begun to decline, as of course this type of moon dial shows the exact shape of the moon as it appears in the sky on the day in question.

The minute hands of the last two clocks have developed into the popular serpentine pattern common in the 1765–1790 period. By this latter date brass dials were becoming very much a thing of the past as the japanned dial replaced them almost everywhere. However some areas retained the traditional brass dial—notably London itself, Scotland, and parts of the

Plate 46. Arched dial clock by Henry Lane of Bristol, *c.* 1780, showing not only the moon's age, indicated by the Arabic numbers in the arch, but also the time of high tide by means of the Roman numbers. Here it is the sixteenth lunar day with high tide at 7.30.

West Country. In these areas the japanned dial did take over, but more slowly. The brass dial, which one finds 'out of period' in these areas, is often of the one-piece engraved and silvered type. Such a silvered dial in its case when viewed across a room can barely be distinguished from a plain japanned one. Both tend to be more clearly legible than the more elaborate engraved-centre composite dials, but the legibility probably did not matter very much. A customer would buy the kind of clock and dial that he liked, and whether it was easily legible at fourteen feet rather than at ten was hardly likely to make him change his preference. Much more important than legibility was the pleasure and pride of ownership.

Plate 47. Eight-day centre-seconds clock *c.* 1760 by Pointer Baker of London. The centre-seconds feature and the engraved centre are both uncommon on London-made clocks. Strike/silent work in the arch is a common London feature.

7 Clocks with Painted Dials

*clocks with . . . enamelled dial-plates, very strong and beautiful, that will
never stain or tarnish . . .*

(From an advertisement of 1782.)

———◆◆►———

The first white dials—who made them and how—'at the same price' as brass dials—
movements made to fit the dials—the falseplate—recognising handcraft from
factory work—some examples, Sam Deacon, Jonas Barber, Henry Bunyan, Robert
Rowntree—rocking figures and moon dials—original price-list—cheap rubbish

Early British clocks always had brass dials. In the third quarter of the
eighteenth century there were a few attempts of an experimental nature at
making clock dials of enamel, like those of watches. This was not at all
successful; the trouble with enamel was that the heat involved in producing
it was so intense that it caused large metal areas, such as clock dials, to buckle
in the process. Such dials as *were* made were therefore generally done as
composite dials, made up of individual modestly-sized pieces of enamelling
—for instance a circular enamel disc for the numbers and another for the
maker's name in the arch. This meant that the brass arched backing-sheet
(usually called the dialplate) was still needed; such dials were thus very costly
and nowhere near as sturdy and durable as normal brass dials. Longcased
dials of true enamel are therefore extremely rare—bracket clock dials less so.
A great many dials described as 'enamel' are not real enamel at all, but japan-
work, as we shall see.

By the 1760s there appears to have been a determination to improve the
legibility of clock dials, as had been done with watches long before. This

was partly because the dials of the later 1750s and 1760s had undergone (in many areas, principally in the north and not in London) a return to an engraved centre. This fussier centre combined with the increasingly popular centre-calendar hand and sometimes centre-seconds hand meant that it was becoming increasingly difficult to read the time. Add to this the smudgy effect of old silvering with the lacquer 'gone off' and a tarnishing brass surround, and we may get an inkling of why repeating-work was becoming more common.

By 1772 the problem had been resolved. The first manufacturers of the new type of legible dial inserted the following advertisement in the *Birmingham Gazette*:

WHITE CLOCK DIALS

Osborne and Wilson, manufacturers of White Clock Dials in Imitation of Enamel, in a Manner entirely new, have opened a Warehouse at No 3 in Colmore Row, Birmingham, where they have an Assortment of the above-mentioned Goods. Those who favour them with their Orders may depend upon their being executed with the utmost Punctuality and Expedition. NB. The Dial Feet will be rivetted in the dials and such methods used as will enable the clock makers to fix them to their movements.

This is a historic announcement. Fromanteel's 1658 advertisement had changed the pattern of clocks for over a century, and now Osborne and Wilson's was to change things for another century. The two most important landmarks in the history of British clocks were advertisements. By 1772 the first known makers of japanned dials had a warehouse filled with their 'assortment'. This type of dial may have been in production a little earlier, but hardly more than a year or two, so we could safely set 1770 as the start of the white dial. They are usually called painted dials today, but as these first ones were largely white, their name was not inappropriate. The correct term should be 'japanned'—the type of decoration we had seen on clock cases earlier in the century, but simplified into a sort of baked oil-painting process. We do not know exactly how it was done, but several stages are evident. The iron dial sheet was treated with a priming paint, then a white groundcoat (usually a duck-egg green or blue tint rather than pure white), then the hand-painted decoration, then lastly the numbers and purchaser's name and town. The first two coats are believed to have been hardened by a stoving process. It was also used for other items, such as tea-trays.

The result was a clearly legible dial with delicate coloured corner paintings, which must have looked very smart and very much like real enamel, or even like decorated china or porcelain. These dials are sometimes described in contemporary accounts as being of these three materials, though we do not know whether this was done deliberately to make them sound more impressive to the customer, or simply through ignorance of the fact that they were really japanned dials. It probably happened for both reasons. Even today people commonly make the same mistake.

The dial was supplied ready-lettered with the name of the clockmaker who placed the order, or alternatively lettered according to his instructions when placing the order, as some customers liked the novelty of having their own names painted on the dial as proud new owners. It is often difficult now to differentiate between the names of owners and those of retailers, but in cases where a certain 'maker' is recorded by only a single example, it is unlikely that he was a serious clockmaker doing it for a living. A professional made at least one clock a fortnight, literally hundreds over the years.

The situation was a little different in cases where japanned dials were exported—a great many were sent to America—as the importer then intended to re-sell them to a variety of clockmakers, whose names could not be known beforehand. Therefore on American clocks British-made japanned dials were supplied without names; the names were added at point of sale according to the customer's requirements.

John Hoff of Lancaster, Pennsylvania, kept a fascinating record of all the clocks he made between 1800 and 1816, an exceedingly rare type of record, of which no example appears to survive in Britain from this period. In January 1805 he noted that 'Rudy Kaufmann—bespoke an eight day clock, *the dial marked with his name* . . .' Quite a few of his clocks were so lettered. What was common practice in America was less common in Britain, but still occurred now and then. Sometimes a customer had his name lettered around the dial in place of numbers.

Until recently there was a widespread misconception about clocks with japanned dials, which arose partly because many of them bear imprinted evidence of the dialmakers (e.g. Osborne & Wilson) most of whom were in Birmingham. Those who were unable to recognise the signs of individual craftsmanship in the movements of a great many painted-dial clocks deduced that such clocks were Birmingham 'factory' products and, on this evidence, condemned them as unworthy of the attention of a collector or enthusiast.

There was also prejudice against them because they were not as old as the (generally) earlier brass-dial clocks. Most writers on the subject have regarded this development as 'degeneration', though it is very obvious that people of the time saw such things as improvements. To value the very old simply because of its age and to decry the less old is no more than a type of informed snobbery. That which is oldest is not necessarily best.

I have unearthed a lot of information on white-dial clocks. It is possible to analyse various features and reconstruct the costing of such clocks when new in a much more detailed manner than can be done with brass-dial clocks. Because we do not have the same detailed information about brass dials, it is not easy to compare the two types against each other in terms of at-new costings. However, the following advertisement (taken from the *Cumberland Pacquet* of 1782) by John Benson of Whitehaven, a man then of thirty years' experience in the trade and today recognised as an outstanding craftsman, makes some interesting comparisons:

John Benson (who *makes* all Sorts of Plain, Repeating, Musical and Astronomical Clocks at Reasonable Prices) . . . has an Assortment of the best Japanned Clock Dial Plates which he makes up to any Sort of Clocks *at the same price as* Brass Plates, which is a great Advantage to the Purchaser as they will never want Silvering, but still be the same, keep as well and clean as soon as Glass. Smoke, Steam and Damp does not affect them, which soon dissolves the best Silvering and Lacker that can be laid on Brass—and the Expense of Renewing the Silver and Lacker comes high or the Clock looks bad and more so when they are exposed to the Sea Air; the Japanned Plates are still the same and the Expense saved [my italics].

This maker sets out the advantages of these improved dials, which he supplies '*at the same price*' as the brass dials, and obviously he is trying to impress on his customers that they are getting a bargain in not having to pay more than for a brass equivalent. (This statement refutes the suggestion sometimes made that they were a cheaper substitute for the traditional brass dial, which by the time another ten years had passed was an anachronism only met with on rare occasions or in certain localised regions where tradition died hard.) John Benson's advertisement is also most interesting in showing how the customer selected his dial from an assortment he was offered and how the clockmaker then made a clock purposely for the chosen dial.

An advertisement in the *Belfast Newsletter* of that same year (1782) similarly stresses that the new dials do not tarnish, and also apparently gives us evidence of the first arrival of this type of dial in Northern Ireland. It was placed by a clockmaker, James Wilson (a different man from the Birmingham dialmaker of that name): 'He has also a few clocks with white enamelled dial-plates, very strong and beautiful, that will never stain or tarnish, being the first plates ever imported into this port . . .'

There seems to be no doubt that the white dial was popular with the customers, as is evidenced by its rapid success. There was however an initial resistance on the part of clockmakers, particularly one would imagine on the part of those who performed their own engraving work, since it made engraving obsolete. Conversely one imagines that those clockmakers who could *not* engrave might have taken to the new dial more readily because it made clockmakers more nearly equal, reducing their tasks to movement-making, and the fine engraver lost the edge he might otherwise have had. But there was more to it than that.

With a brass dial the dial pillars (or dial feet) could be fixed almost anywhere, mostly by neatly hiding the rivetted ends behind the chapter ring, although some southern makers simply screwed them through from the dial front, not apparently minding the visible screwheads. (This latter practice always seems very shoddy, yet one sees it on London clocks bearing very famous names.) The dial pillars had to be attached to the movement frontplate where there was no obstruction. With the new white dials there was the difficulty that the dial feet were fixed *before* japanning, hence the clockmaker might be offered dials with ready-fixed feet that could easily foul the movement at an unacceptable position. Before they could market their dials to clockmakers (who could easily have re-designed the layouts of their future movements) the dialmakers had to overcome this difficulty. This they did (as they explain reassuringly in the advertisement—'N.B. The Dial Feet will be rivetted in the Dials, and such Methods used as will enable the Clock Makers to fix them to their Movements') by means of a fixing plate, usually called at the time a 'backplate' but today known as a 'falseplate'. The false plate was supplied attached to the dial. All the clockmaker had to do was to fix short dial feet to the falseplate by which to attach it to his movement, and as he could determine the positions of the falseplate feet, there was no problem of their meeting his movement frontplate at an awkward spot.

In reality it is rather more complicated than this because of the problem of seconds and calendar features, but this explains the general principle. Thirty-hour white-dial clocks do not have falseplates (except in particular cases for special reasons), probably because they have only three dial feet as opposed to four, and because a thirty-hour has more spare frontplate space than an eight-day movement.

If the clockmaker selected his dial first and then made his movement to fit it (as e.g. we know John Benson did), then of course there would be no problem at all, and no real need for a falseplate. This was obviously the sensible way of going about the job. We know from inventories that some makers kept a stock of dials and made up the movement as needed, just as John Benson did. This method probably explains why quite a number of early white-dial clocks do not have falseplates.

A 'factory-made' japanned dial, then, was usually bought by the 'clock-maker' from a factor such as Osborne and Wilson, and is *not* a sign that the movement also came from that source. However, although this is true of the situation up to about 1800, maybe even till 1820, by about 1825 it is generally true that most 'clockmakers' had stopped making clocks themselves and were buying in more and more as ready-made parts, just carrying out the finishing work and assembly themselves. Therefore in the case of a clock of say 1840 with a japanned dial, it is quite probable that the whole thing, dial and movement, came from a mass-producer and that there is little or no handcraft element in it.

So there is some truth in the old belief that painted-dial clocks were factory-made. To be able to decide how far it applies to an individual clock, one has to have some experience of the movements and to judge each individual case on its merits. If one can see the scribe-marks, where the clockmaker scratched out the wheel positions when setting out his clock train, this obviously indicates a hand-made movement, for a mass-producer did not need scribe-marks; he simply drilled all his plates identically. The presence of a falseplate is also likely to be a signal that a hand-made movement lies behind, because if a retailer were buying a movement complete with a dial then the manufacturer would have no need for a falseplate as all his movements would be designed to fit his range of dials exactly. This guide is not inflexible. Up to 1800 one can be fairly safe in expecting to find a hand-made movement; in the period 1800–1830 mass-production increasingly takes over, and after 1830 it is unusual for anyone still to be making such clocks by hand, unless maybe for some special job such as a regulator.

Plate 48 shows one in position, in this instance on an unusual oval-shaped dial with moonwork at the top. The falseplate can be seen directly behind the moon dial, attached to the dialsheet itself by short feet, with short feet from the falseplate pinned inside the movement frontplate. This dial and falseplate are by James Wilson of Birmingham. The movement is by James Lomax of Blackburn, made *c.* 1785–1790, and is obviously a hand-crafted

Plate 48. Falseplate fitting shown in position between the movement and dial plate. Dial and falseplate were supplied together (in this instance by James Wilson of Birmingham) to simplify the attachment by the clockmaker of his movement. Notice the typical splashes of paint behind the dial, believed to have resulted from careless handling during manufacture.

movement, as is shown by the presence of a falseplate, the unusually shaped movement-pillar outline, the unusually shaped wheel collets, and the scribe-mark on the hammer-arbor. Notice the splashes of white base-paint on the back of the dial, characteristic of very many japanned dials and presumably caused by carelessness in handling the dials after dipping into paint and before drying.

Plate 49 shows a newly-restored dial of an eight-day clock by Samuel Deacon of Barton in the Beans, Leicestershire, a fine craftsman and one of my favourite makers. The dial was made by James Wilson of Birmingham, one-time partner of Thomas Osborne (see page 129). (The partnership broke up at the end of 1777 and Wilson carried on in competition with Osborne until he died in 1809). I would have guessed the age of this clock as about 1780–1785 by the dial style; in fact, Samuel Deacon obligingly numbered and dated his clocks—this one is no. 338, made in February 1789.

With experience a Wilson dial is easily recognised. The two flower sprays inside the inner circle are a little unusual for him, but the rest (corners, arch design, numbering, cut-out calendar) is all absolutely typical. (Not that Wilson made each dial personally—he probably employed a considerable workforce, including perhaps a dozen girls who sat in rows at worktables each painting her particular portion of the dial designs, probably one doing the gold cornerwork, another doing black flower-stalks, another pink flower-heads, and so on; an early production-line system.)

I always call these early Wilson dials (and other similar ones such as Osborne's) 'strawberry corners', because they very often have strawberries as corner motifs. Sometimes they have carnations, roses, or other flowers. Almost always they are delicate, pink things on a white ground. Some describe them as 'feminine' dials. From about 1770 to the end of the century there is little variation and most japanned dials are of this general character.

Plate 50 shows some details of Deacon's movement, the like of which no factory ever produced. Those very beautifully shaped baluster pillars are an extremely rare feature on clocks from this 'late' period. Signs of the engraved name and number are just discernible on the frontplate. Notice the solid great-wheel in the upper centre with a ratchet spring contained within its hollowed rim. Notice too the lifting-piece in the bottom right-hand corner, which is deliberately shaped by Deacon into the form of a bird; its eye is one pin, its long tail forms part of the repeating system. Every detail of the movement is immaculately made and finished, in contrast with some thirty-hour Deacon clocks that are very ordinary. It is interesting to be able to

Plate 49. White dial eight-day clock by Samuel Deacon of Barton, Leicestershire, made in 1789 and numbered 338. The dial was made by James Wilson of Birmingham and is typical of his style, with delicate flowers for decoration. A good-quality dial.

recognise this easily as Deacon's own work, very different from a 'factory' movement.

The Deacon dial was newly restored. Plate 51 shows a thirty-hour dial of similar age from a clock by Jonas Barber junior of Winster, numbered 1060 and made c. 1778 (we can tell within a year or two from the number). This is a superb example of what in the trade is sometimes called 'a sleeper', which is an item which has been untouched for a very long time, perhaps since it was made. This one has obviously original hands and is deeply impregnated with the smoke and grime of two centuries. Notice all the craze marks in the japanwork—these dials often craze that way. The Deacon dial was crazed too, but what shows in fact is the dirt in the cracks and the Deacon one, having been cleaned, does not show the craze lines so obviously.

The Barber dial was probably made by Thomas Osborne. Wilson dials often have a gold border round the flowers (as on the Deacon example), while Osborne's have this less often. It is another 'strawberry corner' type, though of course not with actual strawberries. One of the attractions of such an untouched dial is that no-one has tampered with it; though it is grimy, at least what one sees of the decoration is exactly what was put on when new, not the clumsy work of a heavy-handed restorer. Good restorers for these dials are very hard to find; it is easy to understand and sympathise with the view of an owner who would never dream of having it restored, whereas with brass dials there is little merit in the retention of tarnish.

Until the very last few years of the eighteenth century, japanned dials always had the same numbering system (see the two examples in plates 49 and 51), which was to have Roman hours with Arabic minutes marking 5, 10, 15, etc. and dotted minutes in between. By 1800 and during the next ten to twenty years a change to marking the hours with Arabic numbers took place, often accompanied by a change from dotted minutes to a full minute band, and increasingly by ceasing to mark the minute numbers at all. In the transition period minute numbers were often marked just at the quarter-hours—15, 30, 45, 60. Of course, with the public increasingly familiar with reading

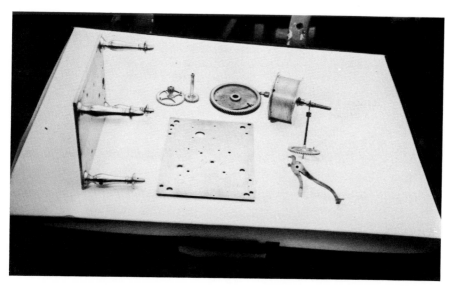

Plate 50. Some parts of the Deacon movement, showing very distinct signs of individual workmanship—unusual pillar shapes, unusual solid wheel, frontplate engraved with his name, serial number and date. Notice that part of the strike-work (right foreground) is shaped deliberately into the form of a bird—evidence of the maker's exceptional pride and pleasure in his work.

Plate 51. An example of a two-hundred-year-old thirty-hour white dial in unrestored condition from a clock by Jonas Barber of Winster, *c.* 1778. The dial is probably by Thomas Osborne of Birmingham. This contrasts strongly with the appearance of the restored Deacon dial in plate 49, page 136. The time-worn state of many such dials has meant that until recently few collectors have taken an interest in these clocks. Once having done so, they are often surprised at the fine quality of workmanship in the movement—as in this instance, for Barber was a fine craftsman.

clock dials, there was no real need to number the minutes. By 1800 the minute numbers gradually began to be omitted, and by 1830 they had pretty well gone.

Plate 52 shows a dial from this period, about 1800–1810. It has the tumbling numbers in Arabics, i.e. they reverse from 4 to 8 inclusive and switch back again from 9 to 3. There is a mark for five past and a mark for ten past, but the fifteen-minute number still on the quarters. This dial has another interesting feature in that the whole of the square surround outside the white numbers circle is done in an Adam-blue background with raised gold spandrel-type corner decorations. This is an unusual treatment and comes in with the new century. In the arch is a painted scene, and very neatly painted too when compared with some of the poor work of twenty years later. It shows a gentleman and a lady on a see-saw with a rustic back-

Plate 52. A costly type of automated dial by F. Byrne of Birmingham from a clock by Henry Bunyan of Lincoln, c. 1800. The couple on the seesaw rock up and down as the clock ticks. The hour numbers are here represented by Arabic numerals, which became popular for a short spell of twenty years or so at the beginning of the new century. A fine dial.

Plate 53. Magnificent and highly ornamental case housing the Henry Bunyan clock. It is made in mahogany with lavish fretwork, especially the pierced pediment; carved and gilded mould surrounding the glass; chequerwork inlay around the doors; inlaid brass reeding in the pillars with brass caps and bases; inlaid medallions in a thistle motif; and the blind fretted spandrel areas in satinwood. In all, this is a remarkably decorative case and must have been tremendously costly to make, indicating the high regard for Bunyan's white dial clock at the time. It is not necessarily a style that would appeal to everyone, however.

Plate 54. A high quality dial from a clock by Colin Salmon of Dundee made about 1800. The finely painted ship rocks as the clock ticks. The naval theme is continued by anchors in the dial corners surrounded by gold tracery. Britain's naval victories were reflected in the popularity of naval themes about this time.

Plate 55. A good-quality dial (newly restored) from a clock by Robert Rowntree of York, *c.* 1825. Arabic numerals and matching steel hands are typical of this period, as is the absence of minute numbering for all but the quarter hours. The shooting scene in the arch is attractively painted. Such a dial cost sixteen shillings when new.

ground. It is a pretty little painting and, which is even more interesting, the see-saw actually rocks up and down as the clock ticks, an amusing feature for which the customer had to pay a high price—the rocking-figure dials were the most costly of all. There are all kinds of variations, such as swans swimming on lakes, ships rocking on rough seas, blacksmiths striking anvils and lions with rolling eyes.

Plates 56 and 57. Two dials from the mid-nineteenth century illustrating the very cheap seven-shilling dial that typified the 1860s and 1870s. Often, as here, they are very badly painted, the figures lifeless and misshapen, the symbolism crude. That by J. C. Elliott of Leeds shows Little Bo Peep; John Waite's of Bradford has the four continents with the Garden of Eden in the arch. At this time there was a mania for religious dials, probably arising from the religious revival of the time (today religious dials are 'death' in the trade). Notice the return to Roman numerals with no minute numbering at all, a feature popular from about 1830-1870.

These rocking figures are pushed back and forth by power from the swing of the pendulum, and technically are therefore interfering with its swing and can have a detrimental effect on timekeeping. However most longcase clocks are such good timekeepers, compared with any other sort, that they take this sort of interference in their stride and I have never noticed erratic performance from rocking-figure clocks.

This clock (by Henry Bunyan of Lincoln) is very fine, and we can see by its case (plate 53) that it was very highly regarded when new, having such a fine and very costly case made for it.

Plate 55 shows the very attractive dial of a clock by Robert Rowntree, who worked in York between 1822 and 1834. It dates from about 1825 and is illustrative of the prettier dials of this period and of the 15, 30, 45, 60 numbering scheme.

143

Below is a known price-chart of japanned dials of the type supplied by James Wilson, that is, good quality later eighteenth century dials. They were sold by size and according to extra workmanship in the way of extra features such as moon dials. These are net trade prices to the clockmaker.

	s. d.
Eleven inch square	8.00.
Twelve inch square	10.00.
Twelve inch arched	14.00.
Thirteen inch square	12.00.
Thirteen inch arched (design in arch)	14.00.
Thirteen inch, landscape in arch*	16.00.
Thirteen inch, moon in arch*	22.00.

(*=eight-day, the rest are thirty-hour dials)

By the 1830s there was a bigger choice of suppliers, though the quality generally was a little lower. Messrs Mabson of Birmingham, for instance, supplied a fourteen-inch thirty-hour arched dial, without seconds dial, curved cut-out calendar aperture, with seller's name lettered on, at 15s. od. each, or a similar dial for an eight-day including seconds dial at 16s. od. each. However, from Joseph May of Birmingham, you could get a selection of dials at half the above prices. A fourteen-inch arched dial thirty-hour was 7s. 6d., and a fourteen-inch arched dial thirty-hour 'with single figures' (i.e. with figures for hours and no minutes numbered) cost only 7s. od.

Some of these later dials are of very poor quality. Plate 56 shows one lettered with the name of the retailer, John Waite, of Bradford, dating from about 1850. It has the four continents for corner designs (*bottom left* America, *top left* Europe, *top right* Asia, *bottom right* Africa). In the arch is the Garden of Eden with Adam, the Serpent and what have you, all very badly painted. This is the sort of dial that has helped give japanned dial clocks a bad name.

8 Clocks for the Wall

. . . spring timekeepers for shops, counting houses, etc. five guineas and upwards . . .

(Liddall & Sons, Edinburgh, 1834.)

———◄◆►———

Hooded clocks—tavern clocks—the Act of Parliament—a gap in the market—
Cartel clocks—English wall dials—water clocks

Eight-day hooded wall clocks appeared very early in the history of British clocks, were few in number, and are therefore very scarce today. They were in fact an experiment which did not succeed. They blossomed, withered and died within twenty years, but they deserve mention, if for no other reason than that they illustrate a failure on the part of clock design to take account of the knockabout realities of daily life.

The pendulum and plate-frame construction appeared simultaneously *c.* 1658 with Huygens' weight-driven clock, essentially a standing clock to fit into a tall case. This was a novelty in Britain, where those who could afford clocks had them as things that were hung on the wall (with the minor exception of spring-driven table clocks, mainly owned by Royalty.)

There seems to have been some resistance to these new-fangled standing clocks, and clockmakers naturally tried to oblige by offering the new plate-frame clock in a wall-hung version, either thirty-hour or eight-day. It was given a wooden cover for protection and ornament, and this type is now called a 'hood clock' or a 'hooded clock'. It is not known whether any specific term was used at the time to describe this type of clock, but in the eighteenth century and later they were called 'head clocks', head being then the term used for a clock hood.

145

Plates 58 and 59. Hook and spike wall clock by Thomas Stanhope of Preston, Lancashire, *c.* 1730, a transitional type midway between the lantern clock and the longcase. The dial is an ordinary longcase single-handed dial, but the movement is a simplified form of lantern movement retaining the turned pillars. The hook can be seen protruding at the top of the movement whilst a 'spike' is attached below each rear pillar. It was hung on a wall-nail and the spikes kept it steady by digging into the plaster. This type of clock is not uncommon in the South-East, but this particular clock, being a Lancashire example, is an extreme rarity.

The eight-day hooded wall clock was really no more than an eight-day key-wound longcase movement fixed in a wall-hung hood. Such clocks exist by makers such as East and Fromanteel, though they are extremely rare. These earliest hooded clocks were an experiment, and as the weight of two eight-day driving weights, the movement and the hood—amounting to forty pounds or more—was all supported by a single nail, it is easy to see why it failed. In practice the best place for an eight-day longcase movement was in a standing case.

The hooded clock, being of plate construction, may seem unrelated to the lantern clock, but it was the fondness for the wall-hung lantern clock which brought about this attempt at a new eight-day wall clock.

The thirty-hour hooded clock, on the other hand, was much more closely akin to the lantern clock, and it was this fondness for the lantern type which gave rise to the diversity of the lantern clock's thirty-hour descendants. We have already seen (page 34) that the sheep's-head clock was a short-lived development, but there were two more very similar descendants of the lantern clock which are recognisable by their different types of movement. These were the lantern clock movement with a square or arched longcase dial, and the birdcage movement with this same type of dial.

It is important to make clear the distinction between lantern and birdcage movements. They are both covered by the generic term 'posted movements', but the lantern has turned pillars and the birdcage has pillars that are square or rectangular in cross-section. Birdcage pillars can be of brass or steel; the earlier ones tend to be of brass and later ones of steel, but that is purely a difference of technique or economy on the part of the maker. Lantern pillars are shapely, birdcage pillars are straight-up-and-down. Lantern pillars survived longest in those areas where lantern clocks had been popular. Birdcage pillars, being more of a blacksmith job, were produced by the earlier country clocksmiths and later (after about 1770) by provincial makers who were simply of an economical turn of mind. At all periods post-framed movements were almost exclusively the product of southern and eastern Britain, and they are exceptional outside that area.

Hooded thirty-hour clocks of birdcage or lantern type were relatively common in those areas during the earlier eighteenth century, dying out toward the 1770s–1780s and virtually extinct by 1800.

In plate 61 is shown a very neat little hooded wall alarm clock by Peter Fearnley of Wigan, the circular dial measuring about eight inches in diameter.

Plate 60. Birdcage movement of an ordinary single-handed longcase clock of *c.* 1730 (by John Fletcher of Ripponden, near Halifax). It is a simplified form of lantern movement, the brass pillars of the lantern being replaced by square-section iron posts. The trains lie one behind the other, as in a lantern clock.

Plate 61. Hooded wall clock with alarm by Peter Fearnley of Wigan, made about 1800. Hooded clocks from North-Western Britain are very uncommon. This example is in a pine case with architectural pediment.

It is very unusual, because a hooded clock was not a commonplace item in the north-west. It is also unusual because it has a circular brass dial and because of its late date. It was probably made purposely to order for some gentleman's kitchen. The attractive little case is in pine, probably originally painted but now stripped. It is a functional yet a most graceful clock. The dial is circular, avoiding the extra cost and size of the more normal square dial.

It is a timepiece only, with alarmwork (notice the central alarm disc) and a plated movement with an anchor escapement and a long pendulum for accuracy—though not a full one-second pendulum in this instance. It is worth pointing out that a long pendulum can vary considerably in length, and need not be of one-second length unless there is a seconds dial on the clock. Indeed thirty-hour clocks very rarely have an exact one-second pendulum. This clock is of eight-day duration or thereabouts.

The hour numerals are engraved on the brass one-piece dial with Arabic numbers, which is unusual for a brass-dial clock. The normal dial of this period would be a painted one. Perhaps the maker did not wish to place a special order to Birmingham and wait for delivery, as he would do in the ordinary way with painted dials (see Chapter 7). The clock was made about 1800–1810. Fearnley was a well-known Lancashire maker who worked at Wigan from 1776 until he died in 1826 aged 77. He acquired a considerable local reputation, particularly for his longcase clocks, which formed the major output of any northern clockmaker.

A most interesting form of public clock sprang up in the eighteenth century, a cross between an exterior tower clock and an ordinary domestic clock, namely a tavern clock, sometimes called a stage coach clock, used at staging posts and not of course *in* stage coaches. This type of clock is most often referred to as an Act of Parliament clock, by that strange reasoning that seems to be the prerogative of clock lore, because, as everyone hastens to point out, they were made both before and after the Act from which they took their name.

Tavern clocks have several distinctive features, all of which stem from their being designed for use in *public* rooms—taverns, hotels, public offices, in churches even. Some say that they were found also in the kitchens of large houses, but this is probably because some authorities try to relegate everything of less than masterpiece quality to the servants' quarters.

Public clocks need to be easy to read and accurate. Hence the dials of these clocks were so large that even the one-eyed could have read them at fifty paces after an evening's carousing, and they were regulated by the accurate weight-driven anchor escapement. Spring-driven clocks with the unreliable verge escapement were justified only where it was necessary to sacrifice accuracy for compactness, and there was no shortage of space in a public room.

The peculiarly English pastime of whiling away the evening by jostling elbow to elbow in a beerhouse dictated the third criterion, that the clock be out of the way of even the more sober patrons. Hence it hung well up on the wall where it was safe from unwelcome interference—safe not only from jostling but from the practical joker. Tavern use also excluded the dangling pendulum and weights of a hooded wall clock—they had to be enclosed. The publican therefore, who well knew the nature of his customers, insisted that his clock must be big, accurate, out of reach, and not too expensive either.

The tavern clock fulfilled the innkeeper's every expectation. The earlier ones date from the 1740s, sometimes earlier. One exists carved with the legend: 'The Gift of Sir Francis Forbes, 1714.' These early ones tend to have the largest dials, a width of thirty inches not being unusual, though even the later ones commonly have twenty-eight-inch dials. The early dials are made of planks of wood, basically square with a very shallow arch at the top. They soon developed to include a small lower section on which the maker's name was often painted, as in plate 62 which shows a 'black lacquered shield dial timepiece' by Matthew Worgan of Bristol.

This early planked type of dial has been named a shield dial. The case simply follows the dial in outline, but has a projecting trunk below to contain the weight(s) and pendulum, access to regulate it being through a small door in this trunk—exactly like the shrunken door of a longcase clock. Apart from its sheer size the most striking thing about a shield dial is that it is numbered in negative, a black-painted background having numbers in gold (sometimes in white) and often the maker's name to match. The hands are of brass, thus further stressing the black/gold pattern and of course giving excellent contrast for greater legibility. With such very large and heavy hands the minute hand, and sometimes the hour hand too, is extended to counterbalance the weight, thereby easing the load on the movement.

The cases of these early tavern clocks are virtually always of the painted type with gold highlights on a black ground, or of Chinese lacquer work (on oak or pine) on a black base. A case of this Chinese lacquer work is sometimes said to have been 'japanned'. Chinese signifies style; 'japanned' the process. It has been stated, though without proof so far as I am aware, that clock cases were sometimes sent out to the Far East for japanning, on a journey which involved maybe a ten-year round trip.

That some of these japanned Chinese cases were English is evident from the fact that some have English prints pasted onto the door and 'worked in' by merging the colour into the black background. One finds this treatment occasionally on the doors of lacquered longcases and I always associate this fashion with East Anglia and the south-eastern corner of the country, though I have come across the occasional example from elsewhere. Both case and dial 'matched' on these earlier examples, being a blend of gold highlights on a black background. The case itself would be about 4 ft 6 in to 5 ft tall.

The eight-day anchor-escapement one-second pendulum movements were almost the same as in a longcase clock but with some variations dictated by the innkeeper's needs. To get an eight-day run into a short weight-fall it was found necessary to add an extra wheel, that is to make the clock into a five-wheel train as opposed to the normal four of a longcase movement. It consequently required a driving weight heavier than the normal longcase twelve pounds or so, and tavern clocks are commonly driven by a weight of around sixteen pounds, even up to twenty-eight pounds on occasion. That meant a tremendous strain on a wall-mounted clock, and it is probably because of this that most tavern clocks do not have strikework, thereby saving a further 16–28 lbs of weight. (Non-striking clocks are known as timepieces).

Even without strikework these clocks led a dangerous life and are not very commonly met with today, though low production may be one reason for this. It is also evident from examination of some of these clocks that they suffered from an obvious design failing. A weak or frayed weight-line could result in the heavy weight dropping free, the consequence being that the falling weight tore the clock from the wall and dashed it to pieces on the tap-room floor, or the clock remained firm on the wall and the weight tore a hole through the base of the case.

The absence of strikework meant that only half of the normal movement-plate area was used. This would have been wasteful of brass, and it is probably from reasons of economy with this very costly metal that most tavern clocks have plates that taper inwards towards the top, sometimes called A-plates. Longcase and wall-fixed regulators are also usually non-striking and they too often have A-plates.

The earlier shield-dial types were soon followed by the occasional octagonal dial but more frequently by circular dials, still with gold lettering on black backgrounds and matching cases. The circular dial left less space for the maker's name, and in these clocks the name was usually lettered on the case itself in the gap between the door and the dial.

Later developments saw a change to a white dial with black lettering, though these usually still had the gold-on-black case with the maker's name on the case. Some later white-dial examples have polished mahogany cases, and so the name had to be on the dial. Most of the black-dial clocks had dials which were not protected by a glass cover. Later on, particularly with white-dial clocks, a brass (or occasionally wooden) bezel with a glass was fitted, but one normally thinks of Act of Parliament clocks as being unglazed.

The Act of Parliament after which these clocks are named was passed in 1797 and imposed an annual tax of five shillings on each clock, ten shillings on each gold watch and two shillings and sixpence on each silver one. The effect of the Act on the clock and watch industry was catastrophic. In an inquiry William Tarleton, a Liverpool watch magnate, testified that his normal workforce of three hundred had been reduced to half because of the resultant lack of demand, and even these men were working only a three-day week. His normal output of twenty gold watches a year had dropped to zero; his usual twenty silver watches a week was reduced to half, and he could not find a buyer for many of those. Thomas Johnstone, a Preston manufacturer of gold watch hands, had been in the business for thirty years. His sales fell by 75 per cent, his staff was reduced by half down to twenty men, and even 'they had nothing to do when I came away on Friday . . .' And some clock books describe the effect of this Act as trifling! Pitt raised a few extra shillings in taxation and threw thousands of clock and watch workers out of work.

The Act was repealed after only nine months. As the tax ran for only nine months before being lifted, no one actually paid the full five shillings; if you see one of the receipts which survive, you will see that the figure charged for a clock was therefore three shillings and nine pence (three quarters of five shillings).

As to the connection between this Act and the clocks known popularly as Act of Parliament clocks, this is one of the many puzzles of horology. It is possible that the sudden disappearance of privately-owned clocks and watches (as people attempted to conceal their ownership of such things) caused the popular attention to be turned towards tavern clocks for checking the time. For whatever reason, the name stuck, even though clocks of this type were made long before the Act was passed.

Plate 62. Scarce shield-dial black lacquer Act of Parliament clock, *c.* 1755 by Matthew Worgan of Bristol. The wooden planks which form the dial are clearly visible. Note that the large hands are both counterbalanced.

Plate 62 shows a clock by Matthew Worgan of Bristol. Its thirty-inch shield dial is made from vertical oak planks painted black with gold numbering, name and decorations. The joints in the planks can be seen plainly in the photograph. This clock is typical of the rather rare earlier style of tavern clock. Its movement has the usual five-wheel train and this one runs on just over sixteen pounds of weight. Its total height is fifty-nine inches. Both the brass hands are counterbalanced. The maker is known to have worked in Bristol after his apprenticeship there (1741 to about 1748). His business probably began there in 1750, when he was admitted as a burgess. The style of the clock suggests it is from his earliest working years. He died in March 1798, only a few months before the Act was repealed.

The second example (plate 63) is of a more conventional type with black circular dial and gold numbering, made by Thomas Daws of Northampton.

Plate 63. Black lacquer Act of Parliament clock with the more conventional circular dial, this one made about 1760 by Thomas Daws of Northampton. The 'w' in Daws resembles a modern 'n', a frequent cause of the misreading of clock signatures.

The black and gold lacquer case shows the 'ears' typical of these circular dials, the projecting pieces at each side of the name. The movement has a typical five-wheel train and A-plates. The maker is known to have worked from 1745 till his death in 1773, and this clock probably dates from about 1760 or a little later. The longer minute-hand is counterbalanced. The dial is thirty inches across and the case fifty-eight inches high. Occasionally tavern clocks have a trunk that is fiddle-shaped, that is one which swells outwards towards the lower section.

Tavern clocks are scarce; like the lantern clock, they were to a great extent localised in region. This is a point generally not appreciated, but it is important because it reflects the considerable difference in clock tastes between north and south. Like the lantern clock they were made in London and the surrounding counties, and while they spread out to cover a larger area than

Plate 64. Cartel clock made by Storr and Gibbs of London in 1741, an exceptionally early date for a clock of this type. The wooden case is gilded and numbered XVII, though the casemaker is unknown. The slit below the XII carries a mock pendulum bob.

the lantern did, they never really penetrated the far north and west. Very few seem to have been made north of a line from Birmingham to the Wash. They are associated particularly with East Anglia, Norfolk, Suffolk, Essex and, of course, London.

The main problem with weight-driven wall clocks (lantern clocks, hooded clocks and tavern clocks) was that the driving weights placed a great strain on the wall mounting. It is therefore strange that it does not seem to have occurred to clockmakers to make spring-driven wall clocks—the obvious

Plate 65. An English dial clock or spring dial, made *c*. 1770 by Hedge of Colchester.
The brass dial is engraved and silvered for clear legibility.

solution to the problem—until the mid eighteenth century. The only
exception was the bracket clock, which was a wall clock in a sense, in that
it might stand on a wall-mounted bracket. Otherwise clockmakers failed to
fill this gap in the market until about 1740.

Plate 64 shows an English carved and gilded wooden-cased wall clock
based, it is generally believed, on the French concept—called a cartel clock,
the word cartel meaning 'dial'. The English examples differed from the
French most obviously in being wooden-cased, where the French clocks
were metal-cased. English cartel clocks are uncommon. The one illustrated

Plate 66. Movember of the Hedge wall dial clock (plate 65) showing clearly the verge, crown-wheel and fusee.

is especially unusual since it is not only signed by the makers Storr and Gibbs of London (known to have been working there in 1752) but the case is actually dated (1741) and numbered (No. XVII). It is therefore a very early example of a style more commonly associated with the 1760s. It is a pity we know nothing about the casemaker.

Cartel clocks are virtually always non-striking—they were timepieces, in other words. They therefore have merely a going train, and so the movements must have been very simple and inexpensive to make, amounting really to half of a bracket-clock movement. No doubt the carving and gilding of the case brought the price-level up again. They are of course spring-driven with verge escapement and fusee. They were probably not as accurate as an anchor escapement weight-driven clock.

Cartel clocks are fairly scarce. Probably not many were made; they are really only suitable for the ostentatious setting of a large house, and the delicate carved flowers and rosettes were very easily damaged, which may help to explain why there are not many left.

The cartel clock was a passing fancy, but there was still an unexploited potential market for spring-driven wall clocks. There were situations where the size of a tavern clock was an impediment and where a striking clock would have been an unwanted interruption or distraction; for these situations the spring dial clock was born. It was a wall-hung clock, spring-driven, without strikework (usually) and, since all that was needed was the time, prominence was given to the dial itself. Plate 65 shows a typical English dial clock (or spring dial, or wall dial).

The simple movement is the same as the cartel movement, an eight-day verge with a fusee or sometimes an anchor escapement with a fusee (see plate 66.) The dial takes up all the case front, the case itself being no more than a box to contain the movement. These clocks are reminiscent of old school clocks or a railway waiting room clock. The early ones had brass dials, but those most often seen have white dials. Once conceived, the strain remained pure for over a hundred years. Early examples dating perhaps from the 1750s may have dials akin to those of tavern clocks. In general they began in the 1770s, initially with brass dials, later with painted dials, and they ran on virtually unchanged until late Victorian times, the only difference being that mass production gradually cheapened them in quality.

An amusing type of wall clock is the water clock, which works by means of a canister of water which gradually empties, causing a single hand to register hours on a dial. Despite their crudely engraved brass dials, their seventeenth-century style and such inscriptions as 'Charles Farnsbarns in ye olde town of Bathe', they are all modern, most being made from about 1920 by Pearson, Page, Jewsbury & Co of Birmingham, well known today as the manufacturers of 'Peerage' brassware.

9 Table Clocks

'A spring clock in a tortoise shell case—£40.00.00.' Supplied *16 August 1693 by Thomas Tompion for the Queen.*

———————————◆————————————

Bracket clocks—London monopoly—verge versus anchor—decoration—engraved backplates—casework—balloon clocks—skeleton clocks—double and triple fusees.

Spring-driven wooden-cased clocks are usually called bracket clocks. Some seem to have been made to stand on a matching wall-bracket, but mostly they stood on a table, a sideboard or a mantle-shelf, according to their size and the period involved.

Bracket clocks were always clocks for the wealthier members of society, for they were much more costly than even an eight-day longcase. Consequently we find that their manufacture was confined in the seventeenth century almost entirely to London makers, who catered for this luxury market. As the eighteenth century progressed only a very small proportion of provincial makers tried their hands at them. By 1800 and into the nineteenth century more are found bearing provincial names, but many of these 'late' ones were bought from London and simply had the retailer's name on the dial. A provincial example before 1800 is now quite a rarity, though in most counties one or two makers are known to have produced them when the occasion demanded.

Wooden-cased bracket clocks were first made about the time of the pendulum's arrival—in a Puritan atmosphere. Hence very early ones are somewhat plain or severe, often looking much like the architectural hood

Plate 67. Walnut-cased bracket clock from about 1725 by Barnaby Dammant of Colchester. It has the verge escapement common to all early examples. The carrying handle is an indication of the clock's most important asset—its portability.

of a Fromanteel ebonised longcase clock, though some were in walnut. They were pendulum regulated, but, despite the fact that the anchor escapement had already been invented, these clocks continued in unbroken tradition using the old verge escapement and bob pendulum. Very rarely was a bracket clock made with anchor escapement until after about 1800, after which there seems to have been a great enthusiasm to 'improve' many an early bracket clock by replacing its verge by an anchor escapement.

The anchor escapement was of course a much more accurate timekeeper than the verge, and timekeeping was a field in which bracket clocks failed alongside their longcase rivals. Spring-driven clocks always had the problem of loss of pulling power as the spring ran down. From the start this was compensated to some degree by the ingenious device known as the fusee (see page 16), but even with fusee compensation they were unreliable. The anchor escapement would have improved the timekeeping of a bracket clock, but even though they knew this, most makers retained the verge escapement, because it did not demand such a level site as the anchor, and a bracket clock (which was almost always provided with carrying handles for ease of moving) was much easier to re-start if the levelness of the surface on which it stood was less important. And of course, frequent dusting of the table or surface would mean constant lifting and shifting of the clock's position. An anchor-escapement clock under these conditions can be a nuisance because the owner constantly has to put coins under its feet to level it again after moving. The perfection of the anchor escapement was unsuited to an imperfect world, and so, very sensibly, it was rejected for bracket clocks pretty well until Victorian times, when Victorian and Edwardian restorers, convinced of their rightness in correcting the errors of the past two centuries, set about replacing verges by anchors.

Bracket clocks often had glass panels in the sides and backs of the cases. (Longcase clocks sometimes had glass side-panels too, especially London ones.) The glass side-panels allowed the owner to see whether the clock lines had run down off the barrels, in which case the clock needed winding. They also displayed the glittering workmanship of the movement, especially, e.g. the turned and finned decoration of the clock pillars.

While in very early examples the pillars were rivetted into the movement frontplates, with pins or latches to secure them behind the backplates and with the outside locking-wheels visible, by the time rack striking arrived it became normal practice to rivet the pillars into the backplate and pin or latch them at the front. These developments left the whole expanse of the

Plate 68. Beautifully engraved backplate of the bracket clock by Barnaby Dammant (plate 67). The border decoration is known as 'herringbone' or 'wheat-ear' design and is typical of the period. A glass door in the back of the case allows the fine backplate to be seen.

backplate unused and visible through the glass panel of the rear door, a perfect opportunity to further display the fine workmanship of the maker by covering the backplate in delicately engraved designs. It is convincingly argued that a maker, who intended a clock to stand on a wall bracket, where the back would be hidden, would hardly waste cost and effort in producing an elaborately engraved backplate. The probable explanation is that such a clock was intended to be put on a table or, perhaps, side-table backed by a wall mirror.

Some seventeenth-century bracket clocks have very beautiful engraved backplates. In the eighteenth century the designs followed the styles of the times, through rococo, Chinese Chippendale and the like, until by the early nineteenth century the engraving was often reduced to a decorative border around the backplate edge, and sometimes also on the pendulum bob itself. Seventeenth-century examples sometimes also carry the maker's signature on the backplate. An early eighteenth-century engraved backplate is shown in plate 68.

Early bracket clocks are superb items; they were made for the wealthy and even today can only be afforded by the wealthy. It was in bracket clocks above all else that the very best makers specialised—men like Tompion, East, Fromanteel and the Knibbs. The top makers delighted in showing how much they could get into such a small space and how ornately they could do so. Not only conventional strikework, but also pull-repeat work, alarms, musical trains, automated figures and moonwork are found in bracket clocks by the best makers.

A feature of many bracket clocks during the later years of the seventeenth century and up to about 1770 was a mock pendulum, that is a curved slit running from about X to II on the dial, behind which a circular disc could be seen swinging from side to side. This mock pendulum was attached by a thin strip to the escapement arbor in the manner of a rocking figure.

Until the nineteenth century it was common for bracket clocks to carry a calendar feature, though very rarely a seconds hand. The dials and hands are very like those of longcase clocks in miniature. Japanned dials were introduced as with longcase clocks, but bracket-clock dials, being smaller, were more easily made of true enamel, and these are met with.

Casework on early bracket clocks, as mentioned above, resembled the hoods of ebony or walnut longcase clocks. By the time of the marquetry period the exhuberance of longcase clocks is reflected in the cases of bracket clocks too, though showy marquetry cases were never very popular for

Plate 69. Bracket timepiece (non-striking) with pull-wind alarmwork on two bells by John Gibson of London, *c.* 1770. The alarm setting-disc can be seen in the centre of the one-piece brass dial. The case is of mahogany with brass trim.

Plate 70. Regency bracket timepiece with japanned dial by James Smith of London, *c.* 1825. The case is restrained in style and is of rosewood with brass inlay and brass grilles at the sides. Side-mounted carrying handles are typical of the period.

Plate 71. Regency mahogany bracket clock with japanned dial by James Ferris of Poole, *c.* 1820. The lancet-top style, lion-mask handles, brass ball feet, brass side-frets and geometrically designed satinwood stringing are all features typical of this period.

bracket clocks. The same applies to lacquered cases. With bracket clocks, however, there was always a far greater tendency for the style of the case to be restrained, if not actually plain. Here we have to exclude (for instance) tortoiseshell cases and those obviously opulent cases with much giltwork made for very wealthy customers. In general bracket clocks retained the ebony/ebonised case style, elaborated when required by a small amount of gilded brasswork, such as escutcheons, handles, and even just fretted plaques. Some early ones were veneered in real ebony, though this soon gave way to ebonised pearwood. (The available ebony supplies are said to have run out by the end of the seventeenth century). By the mid eighteenth century mahogany cases replaced the ebonised ones, often still in fairly restrained and simple style, and here again the simple mahogany case had a long run of popularity. By Regency times mahogany bracket-clock cases often had brass inlaywork as an alternative to inlay of satinwood, and about this time rosewood became popular, sometimes on its own, sometimes with brass inlay, sometimes mixed with mahogany.

The square dial went out of fashion for bracket clocks more or less permanently once the arched dial arrived. By the late eighteenth century an occasional circular dial appeared, and with this new dial shape the case top itself often became a simple dome. Circular dials became increasingly more common, until by about 1820 most bracket clocks had circular dials of either brass or enamel.

One type of circular-dial bracket clock is called a balloon clock, for obvious reasons. An example is shown in the Gillows' drawings (figure 13), though this one is a simple example and balloon clocks are often of a taller and more slender outline, narrower at the waist and with a carrying handle at each side, not on top. Usually they are in mahogany with a certain amount of satinwood stringing, and have a brass bezel round the glass door. Most date from about 1785 to about 1815.

An interesting variation of the table clock developed in the early nineteenth century. The skeleton clock is basically nothing more than a simplified bracket-clock movement, but with no wooden case. Instead the clock plates are cast in a decorative manner with skeleton treatment—that is, as much as possible of the plates is cut away, leaving piercings through which the whole of the operation of the movement can be observed as the clock runs. Plate 72 shows a typical example dating from perhaps 1860–1880. They are rather hard to date precisely because most examples are unsigned and there is no obvious progression in style. They were most popular between about 1870

Plate 72. Typical mid-nineteenth-century single-fusee skeleton clock with pierced chapter ring and passing strike of one blow at each hour. The power for running and striking comes from the single-coiled spring housed in the cylindrical case positioned in the lower centre area.

WALKER's _original_, CLOCK-LAMP, _improved_.

Being fo compleat and artfully contriv'd, that it fhews the Hours of the Night, and anfwers the Ufe both of Clock and Candle: Alfo the Patent profitable Candleftick; with very great Choice of the new-fafhion'd French Plate; and alfo good Choice of the neweft-fafhion'd Stove Grates; and all Sorts of Brafiers and Iron-mongers Wares, and will fell at the loweft Prices, being the Maker, and defigns to make but few Words: Alfo the beft Sort of Town-made Knives and Forks, fine Scif-fars, fine Steel Snuffers, and great Variety of Steel Toys. He likewife makes a very convenient Furnifh'd Candleftick, for pre-ferving the Eyes of thofe that write and read by Candle-light

All fold by J. Walker, at the Brafier's Shop by Cheapfide Conduit: The Clock-Lamps are likewife to be had with proper Oil for them.

N. B. He hath great Choice of Hangers and Swords in the French Plate, which he fells very reafonable; likewife feveral Sorts of Chamber-Lamps in Brafs

Plate 73. An advertisement from _The Country Journal_ (or _The Craftsman_) by Caleb Danvers, published 25 August 1733. This is an improvement on the marked candle idea. This lamp-clock would seem to have an oil-filled tube; as the oil burned so the reading would lower. One presumes, because of the calibration, that if you went to bed after ten o'clock you would have to pour out oil to reach the appropriate level. If you retired before ten, then the clock would be of no use to you. This is not strictly within the realm of clock-work, though its 'inventor' was a maker of clocks.

and 1890. Great play was usually made of the dial, making it a skeleton (i.e. pierced) chapter ring and giving the whole clock a Gothic look.

Most examples, as with the one illustrated, were single-train movements, known usually as single-fusee, in other words like _half_ of a bracket clock. Such a single-fusee example has of course no separate striking train, and often, as with the one illustrated, they were made to perform what is known as a 'passing strike', that is to strike a single blow on the hour (sometimes also on the half hour). The hammer is usually, as here, made in a decorative battle-axe shape. The four turned feet usually bolted into a marble base and the whole clock was then covered by a glass dome (not shown in this example). The dome not only kept the dust out, but also helped prevent the clock tarnishing.

Skeleton clocks are amusing as they enable the observer to watch the wheels turning and to see it all happening. More complex examples sometimes have two trains, as with a bracket clock; these are known as double-fusee clocks, and of course count out the strike of each hour. Even more complex versions can be quarter-chiming or even musical, and these usually have triple fusees. It became fashionable, especially with the more complicated clocks, to make the plates in the form of a church, with the appropriate spires and towers, and some indeed were modelled on particular churches— e.g. York Minster. These were usually double-fusee or triple-fusee clocks.

Many of these skeleton clocks were mass-produced, or at least were sold to the local retailers as ready-made kits. Well-known suppliers to the trade were John Smith & Sons of Clerkenwell, London, and Haycocks of Ashbourne, Derbyshire, who offered a whole range of dial and frame patterns and sold them both as components and as complete clocks. Many of their designs are recorded and skeleton clocks can often be traced to their designs, though they may bear the engraved nameplate of a local retailer. The owner of such a clock would be well advised to read Royer-Collard's book, *Skeleton Clocks*, where many such standard patterns are shown, as well as far more spectacular examples.

10 Casework

James Hue, joiner & gilder, at the sign of the Eagle, immediately within the Netherbow Port, Edinburgh, gilds and japans after the newest form and genteelest fashion all sorts of joiners work, such as clock cases, corner cupboards, dressing boxes, tea-tables, all at very easy rates.

(Caledonian Mercury, 31 March 1741).

Ebonised cases—walnut—mahogany—Sheraton—Gillows' case designs—simple provincial casework—varnish, glasses and finials

The first clock cases were the brass boxes within which the wheel trains of lantern clocks were held. Wooden cases appeared with the arrival in about 1658 of Fromanteel's longer-duration movements with heavier driving weights, at which time a new situation faced the clockmaker. He had to turn to a different tradesman, a woodworker, for his cases. Casemaking was thus divorced from clockmaking, and with very rare exceptions remained in the hands of a separate craftsman from that time on. No doubt the earlier cases were made to measured designs supplied by the clockmaker, but as the clock casemaker gradually evolved as a distinct trade, it was probably increasingly he who was responsible for the design, based on vague specifications from the clockmaker or perhaps the customer—for the customer seems very often to have been the one who chose and ordered the case.

The earliest longcases were 'ebonised'. Sometimes this was done by using ebony veneered onto an oak or pine carcass; sometimes it was pearwood stained black, and sometimes oak or pine stained black. Only from the early 'Fromanteel period' of about 1658–1690 may we expect to see ebonised cases on London clocks. Provincial ones were so few and far between at this

Plates 74 and 75 (*overleaf*) The case of
the John Greenbanck clock (plate 22,
page 90), in early architectural style
in oak veneered with ebony, makes an
interesting comparison with the London version by Fromanteel in plate 5.
A provincial example such as this is
exceedingly rare. Notice the panelled
effect produced by beading.

Plate 76. Ebonised pine case of the clock by James Jordan of Chatham (plate 38, page 116), standing about six feet six inches. Typical of the period is the canopied top, lenticle glass and half-round beading in the long slender door. Such cases are hard to find in good condition. This general style of case can also be found in walnut, but not in mahogany, for this style was outmoded by the time mahogany came into general use.

Plate 77. Ebonised pine case, *c.* 1720, containing a single-handed clock by James Mogg of Basingstoke. The barleysugar pillars and whole general style are more often found in walnut examples.

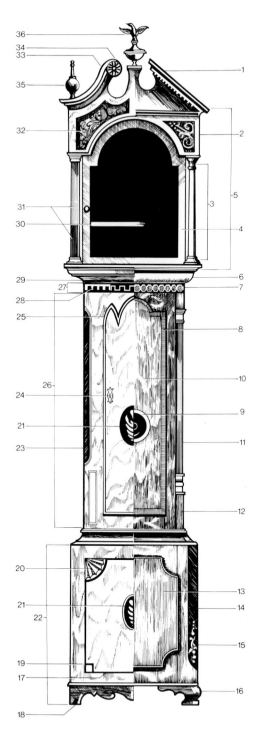

Fig. 11. Casework terminology. This drawing illustrates various casework features which may be met with in widely varying regions and periods. *1*, pitched pediment with dentil moulding beneath; *2*, spandrel area on case, here containing a fret; *3*, pillar caps and bases; *4*, hood door; *5*, hood (or head); *6*, convex (early) moulding; *7*, fret in the impost; *8*, crossbanding on door; *9*, lenticle glass; *10*, counter-matched veneers on door; *11*, reeded quarter column; *12*, pedestal under quarter column; *13*, base panel; *14*, canted corner; *15*, applied carving; *16*, ogee bracket foot; *17*, stringing line; *18*, semi-French foot; *19*, broad crossbanding; *20*, fan inlay; *21*, shell inlay; *22*, base (or pedestal, in old terminology); *23*, canted corner with stringing; *24*, escutcheon; *25*, gothic top; *26*, trunk; *27*, impost; *28*, dentil moulds (*left*, plain; *right*, key-pattern); *29*, concave moulding; *30*, seatboard; *31*, pillar, reeded and double-reeded; *32*, inset painted glass panel; *33*, swan-neck or scrolled pediment; *34*, carved rosette; *35*, finial—spire type; *36* finial—eagle type.

time that one can make no observation. As the provinces therefore missed this ebonised period, it is not at all surprising to find ebonised cases twenty or even forty years later as an occasional form. The case of the John Green-banck clock (plate 74) represents a provincial case in the simplified London form, but perhaps ten years or more out of period. Provincial ebonised cases were by no means always of the Fromanteel architectural type, but may have been of the style and shape more usually found in oak or walnut. Plate 76, for example, shows an ebonised pine case in a style associated with walnut.

Gradually walnut veneer began to replace ebony in London, culminating in the spectacular marquetry cases of the late seventeenth and early eighteenth centuries. The provinces to a certain extent also missed the walnut period, because at this time there were few eight-day clocks, though such few as there were are usually found to have had the London-type walnut or even walnut marquetry case. Most early provincial clocks, being thirty-hour clocksmith work, had simple cases in oak, sometimes in pine, though of the latter there are few survivors from before the mid eighteenth century; thus surviving provincial cases made before 1750 are usually of oak.

By the mid eighteenth century mahogany was being shipped into Britain in sufficient quantities to be widely available. Its popularity developed earlier in western Britain, perhaps because it was shipped in through such ports as Bristol and Liverpool. Early mahogany was heavy, of a dark brown colour, nearly black at times, and was used in the solid. This was from Cuba and the Spanish West Indies, and is often termed 'Spanish mahogany'. Later in the century a paler type was imported from Honduras and this was used more in veneered form, as it would have been wasteful to use this finely figured wood in the solid. In some areas such as south-eastern Britain plain straight-grain walnut was used into the period 1750–1775, presumably imported from Europe as the finer English walnut stocks were exhausted by the start of the century. Plain-grained walnut was no more costly than wainscot oak (i.e., oak which was quarter-sawn to show the snaky medullary rays), but being prone to woodworm, walnut was far less durable. English oak is almost immune to worm unless softened by, for example, damp floors. Mahogany in the solid was totally immune to worm.

The shades and varieties of mahogany were so numerous that, whether in the solid or in veneer, all manner of permutations were possible. In the west, especially the north-west and Scotland, it rapidly became popular for better-quality casework. While it was a superior wood, it was also costly,

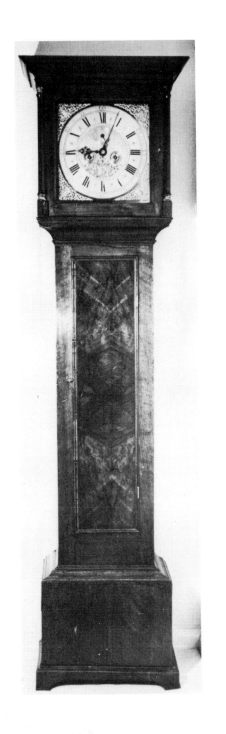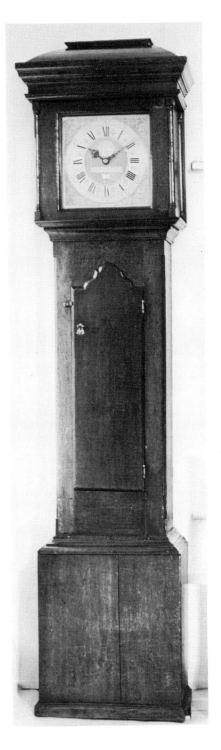

Plate 78. (*far left*). The case of the William Nicholson of Whitehaven clock (plate 39, page 117), illustrates the provincial concept of a walnut case. The wood is here used entirely in the solid except for the door, where two veneered panels are bookmatched to form interesting patterns. Walnut was not used as much in the North as in the South. Height: about six feet six inches.

Plates 79 (*left*) and 80 (*above*). Oak case of thirty-hour clock by William Porthouse of Penrith, *c.* 1750, standing about six feet six inches. There is a primitive charm about some of these simple sturdy country cases. The close-up presents a rather 'dumpy' appearance caused by the over-wide door surround in the hood. Oak dowel pegs show at all the joints. These are very unusual on better-class casework but on cases housing clocksmith-type work they are common, and probably indicate the work of the village carpenter rather than a true casemaker.

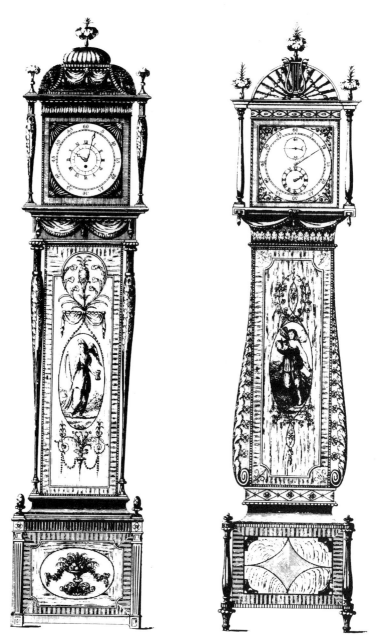

Fig. 12. Line drawing showing Thomas Sheraton's two designs for clock cases published in 1791. Great emphasis is placed on the use of veneers of exotic woods and marquetry work. No examples are known to exist made to these designs, although casemakers did on occasion use isolated 'Sheraton' features. Notice that both of these grand designs are for clocks with japanned dials.

and humbler thirty-hour clocks and eight-day cottage clocks continued to be made to the end of the century in oak. By the start of the nineteenth century mahogany veneer was so widely available that it had become dominant in most clock cases.

Early provincial casework followed to a greater or lesser degree the shapes and styles of London, though sometimes in humbler woods. By mid-century, however, provincial work had blossomed into such a variety of shapes and forms that it is only possible to illustrate a few examples. For the experienced it is very easy to ascribe a period, and often a region, to a particular case, but the multiplicity of shapes can be confusing, and one can only advise a beginner to look at as many examples as possible, in order to become accustomed to the gradual development from the simplicity of provincial work of the early eighteenth century to the elaborateness of the mid nineteenth century.

Figure 12, page 180, shows two famous Sheraton designs, which seem to be an exercise in making wood look like other substances, such as metal, foliage or drapery. Although no examples exist of cases made to these designs, they are not without interest; like Chippendale's designs, they incorporate some exciting and interesting ideas, and must have been an occasional source of inspiration to many casemakers.

Sheraton's influence seems to have been strongest in the north-east, and to a lesser extent in other regions, but to have been distinctly weaker in those regions which favoured the Chippendale style. Sheraton tended to do in inlay what Chippendale did three-dimensionally with moulds, carvings and frets. When a clock case is described as being in the Sheraton style, this does not mean that it resembles the designs shown in figure 12. Plate 81 shows the base panel of a 'Sheraton' clock case showing typically fine inlaywork.

I know of one, and only one, set of detailed records concerning casemaking for British clocks, the estimate books for the cabinet-making firm of Gillows of Lancaster, where minute details with working drawings are recorded of some thirteen patterns of clock cases made by the firm in the late eighteenth century. This is our solitary source for such detailed information on style, terminology, cost and expertise. Compared to the Gillows records everything else is mere speculation. They are therefore worthy of our close attention.

We will examine the drawings shortly, but first let us look at a unique

Plate 81. Base panel of a mahogany case of about 1790 showing features which we designate as 'Sheraton'. A coloured urn medallion in the centre and fan inlays in the corners are framed in a double line of stringing in pale wood.

document. It is a price-list, drawn up in 1785, of optional extras that Gillows journeymen might be called upon to perform for any particular order over and above the straightforward case-pattern. It sets out the rates that Gillows would pay them for each extra, and gives all the contemporary terminology as used by the men who actually did the job. We are privileged to have this unique view of the working of the clock case maker. First is described the basic case, then the optional extras.

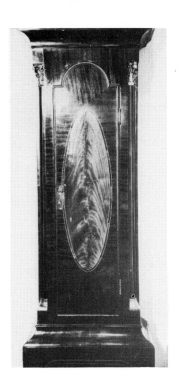

Plates 82 and 83. The door and hood of a very fine Sheraton-style mahogany case of about 1790 from a white-dial clock by Thomas Husband of Hull. The oval panel of superb mahogany is typical of Sheraton influence and is surrounded by a band of crossgrained rosewood within white stringing lines. The quarter columns are also crossgrained rosewood spaced by stringing. The bell-top canopy is centred with a shell inlay. The clock shows moonwork and also tidal times and is an example of the very best in provincial work of the period.

Plate 84. Base of a grand mahogany Liverpool clock of about 1780 showing Chippendale influence in the local taste. The brickwork corners, blind frets flanking the door and raised bookmatched base panel are all features particularly associated with Lancashire casework.

Plate 85. Thirty-hour clock, *c.* 1785, by Lawrence of Lancaster. The plain oak case with mahogany trim is typical of the style of Gillows' cheaper cases. The plain semicircular doortop is a common feature of Lancashire work.

	s. d.
A mahogany clock case with square head, quarter columns in the body, cant'd pedestal veneer'd. Also the body door veneer'd, plain cornice, crossband'd frieze, and moulded [?bragals] ...	15.00.

Add:-

For stringing and crossbanding the doors with arch'd top	1.00.
If the doors be divided into 2 panels and a little moulding overcross ⎱	3.
If the door be strung and crossband'd in 2 panels more than one ⎱	3.
If pedestal be strung	3.
If do. be crossband'd round	6.
If c'ntermatch'd joints in the veneer	3.
If common dentils in the impost [i.e., the band below the hood]	6.
If quarter columns be fluted and returned at ends	1. 00.
If do. flut'd and counterflut'd.	1. 6.
If 4 columns in the head be flut'd and return'd, 4d. ft	1. 4.
If 4 do. be flut'd and counter do. 6d. ft.	2.00.
If pitched pediment return'd common & fixing shield	2.00.
For do. if making	2. 6.

Add:-

For a scroll'd pediment more than a plain top	3. 6.
For dentills in scroll'd pediment	9.
For dentills in pitchd do.	6.
For a frett in cants of pedistall	1. 0.
For a do. under the impost	1. 0.
For arch'd face and plain spandrels	3. 0.
If cut out for plain spandrels	1. 6.
For ... spandrels more than plain	1. 0.
If pedestall under quarter columns be veneer'd	4.
If do. be strung	4.
If do. be not strung but crossband'd	8.
Clock cases with round faces	
One do. with arch'd pediment, quarter columns in corner flut'd thro', cant'd pedestal all veneered cant'd, brackets plain, one joint in front of pedestall, veneer body door in one veneer band'd and strung and arch'd top, frett in the impost, plain columns in the head, the glass door [?] crossband'd and string let in the angles of do.	1. 8.

Add:-

If sides of the head be veneer'd 3d. ft. side [each side?]	6.
If sides of the body be do. 6d. ft.	1. 0.

185

Deduct:-
If side of pedestall be solid, 3d. ft.   6.
Add:-
If the impost be cut and Gothic   1. 0.
If cornice be cut same way   1. 0.
Turn'd Gothic sticks in the corner of the body each
glu'd up in 3 as fluted quarter columns as above
included.
Add:-
If pillars in the head be turned in 4 and glued up to be
more than plain   1. 0.

The drawing of a typical clock case showing named parts in figure 11 may be helpful.

For ease of reckoning let us assume that one penny in 1785 had the same purchasing power as one pound today. Remember that Gillows were supplying all the materals—they had a stockroom full of mahogany, canarywood, zebrawood, etc.; the above are purely labour costs.

Let us now look at the thirteen drawings from their estimate books. We have set them out like a catalogue with very brief details alongside and the estimated retail price calculated on a fifteen per cent profit margin (based on the known profit on case no. 8).

I have put in brackets today's equivalent based on one pound for one penny, just to bring home fully how costly these things were to a purchaser of that period. Remember, too, that these prices bought you only the case— you still had to buy a clock to go in it.

These case prices are of course a lot more than today's going price for these items as antiques. In other words we are still buying our antique clocks cheaply, at second-hand values. No one who studies these Gillows price records can turn round and say that antique clocks are expensive. They are still very undervalued, even compared to the price when new.

The following pages constitute the only eighteenth-century clock case catalogue in the world. They merit careful scrutiny. There are thirteen examples though, as some are costed out in more than one basic wood option, they cover more than thirteen cases. In any event, each pattern would probably have been re-used many times over.

Let us look at the full details of case no. 8, made on 29 January 1791.

a Oak Clockcase Square face.	s.	d.
10½ ft of 1 inch oak at 5d p. ft.	4.	3¼
12¼ ft of ½ inch oak at 2¾d. p. ft	2.	9½
2 ft of 1 inch mahy(mahogany) at 9d. p. ft	1.	6
1¼ ft of ¼ inch mahy at 2½d. p. ft.		3½
2⅓ ft of mahy Vinr. (veneer) at 5d. p. ft		11½
12 ft of ½ inch deal at 1¼d. p. ft	1.	3
5 ft of 1 inch deal at 2d. p. ft		10
1 lock and escutcheon		6½
1 pair of clockcase hinges		4
1 pair of swan neck hinges and a brass button [knob] for glass door		2
Turning pillers, caps and bases, etc		6
Incident[al]s to do.	1.	8¼
Makeing do. Thos Lister* compute	15.	3½
Glass for door cost	1.	9
	£1. 10.	5

Not the clockmaker of that name.

That was the cost. A note below suggests the retail price: '£1. 14s. od. without glass at Preston.' They got the profit on the glass twice, once by charging it in the costing, and then they did not supply it!

Figure 13(8) shows the rough sketch (dimensions were given but are omitted for clarity). And shown in plate 85 is an actual example, obviously made to this precise drawing and presumably by Gillows. The clock this case contained is shown in plate 29, a thirty-hour brass dial signed Lawrence-Lancaster. The clock style suggests the 1780s. The case was not marked with any Gillows stamp—I believe they did 'sign' their cabinetwork after about 1830. This was a very good example of a modest case preserved in perfect condition. The photograph reveals one or two points not immediately obvious from the specifications.

First of all, this was to be an oak clock case. What was the mahogany for, solid and veneer? The photograph shows us: the solid was for the hood pillars, the trunk quarter columns and blocks at their bases, the neat little ogee bracket feet and the mould just above them, all just as crisp and clean as the day they were cut. The half-inch deal was for the backboard. The mahogany veneer was for the hood door and the broad panel just above it. The veneer was also for crossbanding all around the door edge and all around the base panel. No canted corners on this example.

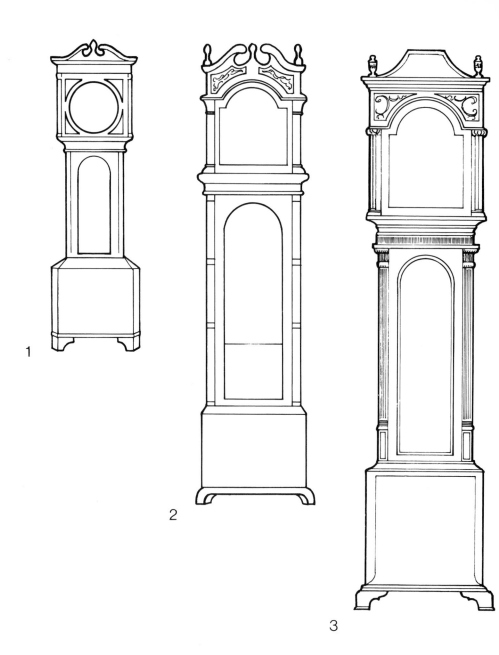

1

2

3

4

5

6

7

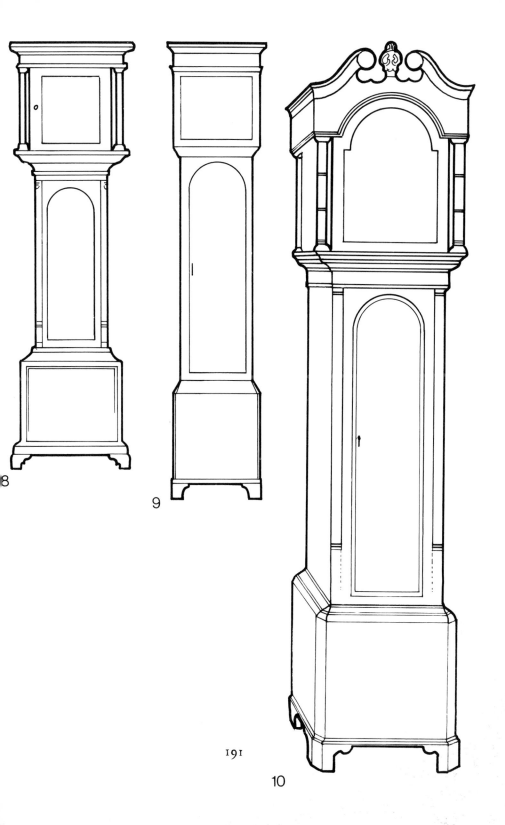

8

9

191

10

11   12

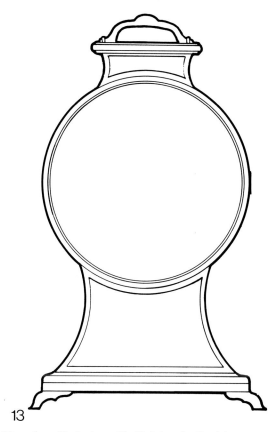

13

Fig. 13 (*pp. 188–193*). *1* Made in 1786. Height 7ft 8in (plus swan-necked pediment). Mahogany. Circular dial, canted corners to the base and feet. The quarter-columns were 'fluted & counter-fluted' by which is meant reeded and double-reeded, in solid mahogany. (London clocks by contrast often had the double-reeding inset as brass between the lower reedings of the pillars.) Cost £3. 0s. 2d.; retail price £3. 9s. 0d. (£828). *2* Made in 1787. Height 8ft 3in. Mahogany. A much more spectacular and pompous case, with extra work involved partly because of the extreme height, partly because of its greater complexity. Cost £4. 12s. 5½d.; retail price £5. 6s. 4d. (£1,276). *3* Made in 1787. Height 8ft 9in; dial 13½in. Mahogany. Cost £5. 5s. 7d.; retail price £6. 1s. 5d. (£1,457). *4* Made in 1787. Height 7ft 9in; dial 13in. Mahogany. Cost £4. 8s. 6d.; retail price £5. 1s. 9d. (£1,221). *5* Made in 1787. Height 8ft 3½in; dial 13in. Mahogany. No price given. *6* Made in 1788. Height 7ft 4in; dial 13in. Mahogany with kingwood bandings. Cost £5. 16s. 10d.; retail price £6. 14s. 4d. (£1,612). *7* Made in 1790. Height 7ft; dial 13¼in. Oak. Cost £2. 0s. 11d.; retail price £2. 7s. 0d. (£564). *8* Made in 1791. Height 7ft 3in; dial 12in. Oak. Cost £1. 10s. 5d.; retail price £1. 14s. 0d. (without glass) (£408). *9* Made in 1795. Height 6ft 4¾in; dial 14in. Deal (painted). Cost £1. 6s. 1d.; retail price £1. 9s. 8d. (£356). *10* Made in 1797. Height 8ft; dial 13in. Mahogany crossbanded with zebrawood. Cost £3. 9s. 6d.; retail price £3. 19s. 8d. (£956). *11* Made in 1797. Height 7ft; dial 13in. Mahogany. Cost £2. 13s. 6d.; retail price £3. 5s. 3d. (£783). *12* Made in 1798. Height 7ft 6in; dial 13in. Oak. Cost £2. 2s. 3d.; retail price £2. 8s. 7d. (£583). *13* Made in 1800. Height 22in; dial 13¾in. Mahogany with canary wood. Cost £2. 11s. 7d.; retail price £2. 19s. 3d. (£711). NB dearer than several of the longcases.

Notice by the way that the base-panel is made from two joined pieces of oak—they have parted slightly. If we recall, the basic tradesman's agreement specified 'one joint in front of pedestal'. Their point of course was '*not more than* one joint' for several joints involved more work, but why a joint at all? Why not one piece of wood, which saved work all round? The answer is that to get one piece of oak wide enough to span the eighteen-inch plus base, would mean using a board taken from a tree at least four feet wide, because of the wastage near the bark and at the centre of the tree, where the soft sapwood could not be used. Of course, there were not that many four-foot wide oak trees around. Sometimes the sapwood was used, and this often shows as paler-coloured yellow bands, particularly prone to wood-worm, while the rest of the hard oak was not.

There is a small difference between the case and the rough drawing—ignoring the proportions—because the sketch is not a measured drawing but simply a rough outline. The case has ogee bracket feet (curved in cross-section); the sketch shows plain bracket feet (flat in cross-section). The ogee ones were better, of course, more graceful, but took longer to make and were therefore more costly, especially in mahogany.

The cases in plates 86 and 87 illustrate clocks by William Parkinson of Lancaster and Thomas Shaw of Lancaster; although we have no proof that they were made by Gillows, I believe that they were. These fine cases illustrate very well many of these features we have seen detailed in the Gillows' workbooks. The first one, by William Parkinson, dates from about 1760. The maker became a freeman of Lancaster in 1758. The second one is actually dated 1777 inside the movement. Shaw was a freeman there in 1766. Parkinson and Shaw was probably contemporary rivals.

Parkinson's clock has canted corners to the base, canted ogee bracket feet and stringing around the solid mahogany door. The hood has carved wooden rosettes on the ends of the scrolls, dentil mouldings along the curves of the scrolls, and the hood pillars are 'reeded and double-reeded' at the lower portions or, as Gillows called it, 'fluted and counter-fluted'.

The Shaw case is somewhat grander, largely because of its later period style. It has reeded quarter-columns to the trunk with stringing in the boxes below them. The base consists of two matched veneer panels and the door is treated in the same manner, but has an astragal moulding round it. The base has canted corners (the feet are in fact missing). There is a wavy pattern of stringing in the 'impost'. The swan-necks also have dentil moulding along them with carved rosettes and the rather unusual feature (for Gillows) of

Plate 86. Eight-day clock, *c.* 1760, by William Parkinson of Lancaster; the case, standing about seven feet six inches high, is believed to be by Gillows. Notice the canted corners with canted ogee bracket feet, the carved rosettes in the swan-necks (which also have dentil mouldings), and the reeded and double-reeded pillars with wooden caps and bases—all typically Lancashire features on higher-quality casework. The convex moulding below the hood is here a throwback to earlier styles and is not a guide to period. This is a good clean example of early Lancashire casework in *solid* mahogany.

fretting below the swan-necks. The hood pillars are 'fluted and counter-fluted'. An extra point on both cases is that the glass doors have ogee moulded frames, a very common Lancashire feature. They are both fine cases and the Gillows workmen would be proud to know they had survived two centuries in such good condition, which in itself must be ample testimony to their skill.

Plate 88 shows a development of the basic Gillows pattern extended and exaggerated in certain respects. This illustrates the grander 'Liverpool' case, typical features of which are the 'brickwork' base, frets on the 'impost' and on the boxes beneath the quarter-columns, glass panels set into the hood below the swan-necks, and double pillars to the hood/hood door. Such cases must have been extremely expensive.

At the other end of the range were the clock cases of ordinary country makers of thirty-hour clocks, men like John Boot of Sutton in Ashfield, Nottinghamshire. Boot set up business there after finishing his apprenticeship with Thomas Binch at Mansfield about 1725. He was the founder of a whole family of clockmakers and worked there until his death in 1767 at the age of 63. Like many provincial makers of his time, his main output was of thirty-hour clocks, brass-dial clocks, of course, at this period, many of them simple one-handers.

What *is* exceptional about John Boot is not only that we know who made his clock cases, but that the account records of his casemaker are preserved and form one of those very rare instances where we can examine the workings of the clock casemaking trade.

The Haslam family of Sutton were local builders, carpenters and undertakers. Their trading accounts survive in the possession of local historian, Mr W. Clay-Dove of Sutton, who has kindly allowed me to use extracts from them.

Plate 87. (*opposite left*) Eight-day clock by Thomas Shaw of Lancaster made in 1777; the case, standing about seven feet six inches, is believed to be by Gillows. Notice the book-matched door and base, canted base corners, stringing design in the 'impost', carved rosettes and dentils on the swan-necks, double-reeded pillars with turned caps and bases and the ogee mould to the hood door—all typical of fine Lancashire work. The fretting below the swan-necks is unusual on Lancashire work.
Plate 88. (*opposite right*) An example of the grander 'Liverpool' case, standing over nine feet tall. This one houses a world time-dial clock by Thomas Lister junior of Halifax, made about 1785. The case is obviously in the Lancashire style, maybe bought by Lister from Gillows. The style of these cases does not appeal to everyone today, but when they were made they were very highly regarded and extremely expensive.

These records are probably unique as evidence (not speculation) of case-making in the more humble realm of country clockwork. There is no question of bracket clock cases, nor even of spring wall clocks, but just simple country longcases, many of them of softwood, probably finished off by painting as with the Gillows pine cases. The records are not detailed. Here are a few sample extracts:

John Boot Account. 1745. *Clockmaker.*	s.	d.
22 Sept had a clockcase	8.	6.
3 Nov ,, ,, ,,	8.	6.
19th Dec ,, ,, ,,	8.	6.
8th Dec had an oak clockcase	13.	6.
26th Dec a clock case	8.	6.
Had a clock weight of me, 11 lbs.		
3 March Had an oak clock case	13.	6.
20th March Had a clock case	8.	6.
6 foot and a half to mend a case	1.10.	
Peter to mend case and nails	1.10.	
1749.		
1st Oct had a clock hed	1.	8.
6th April Had three knobs for Stephen Corton's		
clock hed. He found brass.	1.	3.
1757.		
23rd July. Had a norway case	£ 1. 1. 0.	
17th Sept. ,, ,, ,, ,,	1. 1. 0.	
Made a hors for to set clock on	1. 0.	
10 April. A norway case arch face	1. 1. 0.	
21 June ,, ,, ,, ,, ,,	1. 1. 0.	
Had sixe clock glasses at 1/5 apeese	8.	6.
1759.		
23rd Feb. Had a clock case, arch face for Godfrey Marriott		
26 Apr. ,, ,, ,, ,, ,, ,, Samuel Unwin	1. 4.	6.
22 Dec ,, ,, ,, ,, ,, ,, Samuel Butterworth		

There is more to this than quaint terminology and bad spelling. Where is all the mahogany? Where is all the zebrawood, canarywood, satinwood, inlaying, stringing, carving and gilding and fretting? All are conspicuous by their absence. Haslam's cases came in two types—*the* case or the *oak* case. Softwood cost you 8s. 6d., oak 13s. 6d.—obviously for square dials. For arched dials you paid £1.1.0. in softwood, £1.4.6 in oak. The expression 'norway case' signified not a new fashion from Scandinavia, but that it was made from Norwegian pine.

These seemingly small sums make us smile today, but if we translate

Haslam's 8s. 6d. pine case by our pound-for-penny formula, that makes it £102, which may seem rather high. However, consider that if you could get a craftsman to make you such a case new today at three pounds an hour, and he took three eight-hour days to do it with thirty pounds' worth of timber and materials, that would add up to exactly £102. And that is by no means an unreasonable estimate of time and materials, even with modern machines and tools!

So John Boot had 8s. 6d. plain pine against the £1. 9s. 8d. charged by Gillows for pine; 13s. 6d. oak against Gillows' £1. 14s. od. plus glass. You got three Haslam pine cases for the price of one by Gillows, two and a half oak ones for one from Gillows. That was some price difference. Of course, there is a thirty-year time-lapse, but inflation over the years was only slight. The main difference was one of quality.

Haslam is probably representative of much of provincial work—'Will you have *the* case or the *oak* case, sir?' Just imagine if a customer had approached Haslam with the Chippendale guidebook in his hand. The book itself would have cost more than Haslam's case!

Haslam evidently made clock cases for private customers as well as clock-makers, and this confirms that it was possible for the original customer to buy his clocks either already housed in a case or without a case and then to select one of his own choosing.

Here's an interesting item: '1748. Varnish for a clock case 5d.' Why is fivepennyworth of varnish interesting? Because this is one of the few rare records which *prove* that clock cases were varnished when originally sold. Similarly, on the balloon clock case account in the Gillows records (No. 13) there was a charge of 1s. 6d. for varnishing. Of course, an oak case had to be varnished when new, or the colour, which was often artificially applied (commonly a reddish shade), would simply have rubbed out with waxing, and you would be left with whitish-grey oak about as exciting as a broom handle. Sheraton's pattern book gives the recipe for a stain made from red brickdust to get this rich colour. Those who throw up their hands in horror at the thought of varnish having been used on an antique just do not understand the situation. Varnish *was* used on oak, and apparently on mahogany too (the Gillows balloon clock) to seal in the colour, fill the grain, and provide a hard surface onto which a beautiful patina would build up over the years through waxing.

The 'hors' was of course a 'horse'; i.e., a clockmaker's rigid rack or frame on which he sets up clocks for testing when out of their cases. The prices of 1s. 5d. each for glasses for the hood doors compares with the Gillows prices for square glasses at 1s. 6d. to 1s. 9d. each. However, for their arched dials Gillows sometimes specified what they described as 'fine glass' at 4s. 0d., against ordinary glass at 3s. 0d. All these prices show how very costly glass was, making up about one sixth of the total cost of Haslam's cases.

One of the items I like best is the 1749 entry: 'Had three knobs for Stephen Corton's clock hed. He found brass. 1s. 3d.' The clock 'hed' was what Gillows also called the 'head', but what we nowadays would call the hood. These knobs were, of course, brass finials to decorate the hood top—and look how very costly these were. On Lancashire casework one would tend to find gilded wooden finials rather than brass ones—Gillows usually called the two side ones 'vases' and the centre one a 'shield'. Unfortunately, we cannot break down the actual cost of their finials. But 1s. 3d. for making (?casting) the finials when the customer provided his own brass—again about one sixth of the total just for the finials! Brass itself was always a costly raw material, worked brass even more so.

Even in the nineteenth century, when such items were factory produced, brassware was costly. John Manby, a clockmaker at Skipton, bought finials from the Birmingham brassfounders in the 1830s at 1s. 5d. a set of three for spire type, 1s. 7d. a set of three for eagle type. We call them finials today, but somehow the older terminology has its own charm about it—Haslam called them 'knobs', Manby called them 'clock balls'. One of my favourite entries from the Manby accounts is the £4 2s. 0d. he charged (without a case) for 'a new clock and balls to Mr Lister of Grassington'.

II *Collecting and Investing*

. . . . trade was driven into the hands of those who were not trained, so that there is scarcely a cloth shop or hardware shop that does not deal in watches, who know no more about a watch than a cow does of a new-coined shilling.
(Advertisement of John Begg of Edinburgh,
clock and watch maker, *c.* 1807.)

———————◆▶————————

The average collector—reference books—quality points to look for and to avoid—hints on price-structure according to demand—where to buy—right or wrong—furnishing-pieces—recommended reading list—will it be an investment—inflation—some comparisons in values over the last ten years—quality more important than price—some areas for future investment—pretty cases—the collector/investor

Most collectors I know start off by buying, or by already owning, a single clock, usually a longcase one. Then the compelling fascination of this sort of clock begins to take hold. The collector feels he must get to know more about his clock, so he reads a book or two. Before long he decides he would like a second clock, one to go in the dining room if the first is in the lounge, or a painted dial if his first one has a brass dial, or an eight-day if his first one is a thirty-hour; there is no end to the means by which one can convince oneself of the desirability of owning a second clock—and justify the need for it to one's spouse! Then comes a third clock, then a fourth. In no time at all the purchase of clocks can become a major driving force in one's life. Other antiques soon lose their pull by comparison. There is not really any rational reason, it is simply that clocks do exercise this magnetic hold over one.

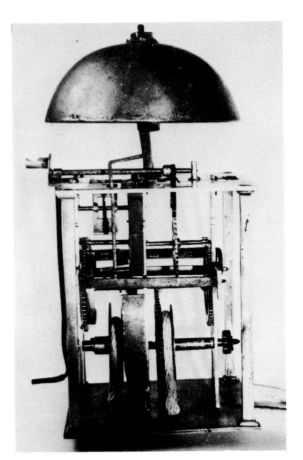

202

If one felt the need, one could always justify their purchase by pointing out the investment aspect, for there is nothing that I know of that has appreciated so much in value over the last ten years as clocks, and most of all British provincial longcase clocks. If you need a financial incentive, then it is there.

Most 'collectors' in my experience are people such as I describe above. They are not people with large pocket books who can buy a hundred clocks, or even fifty clocks, but people who cherish three or four clocks—or maybe a few more, according to their means. I doubt if many of them would feel they justified the term 'collector', nor are they in any sense building up a 'collection'.

Most would think of themselves as beginners; indeed, we are all of us learning more every day. Just as you begin to think you have a certain aspect clearly defined in your mind, there crops up a contradictory example, and you start learning all over again.

All of us, collectors, dealers and enthusiasts, regard clocks to some extent in the way that a train-spotter regards trains. We have to, because the finances involved prevent most of us from owning most of the clocks we see. Even a dealer enjoys looking at the clocks that he does not buy. It is all part of an enjoyable quest. Dealers, however, do not want their shops filled each day with clock spotters.

We enjoy looking at them because each one we see will add to our experience, whether by confirming or by contradicting views we may hold. One thinks of those TV programmes where panellists seek to identify ancient objects: how can they be sure that a certain item is 'German, fourteenth century—made by a man with a limp in his left leg . . .'? But experience

Plate 89 (*opposite top*). Movement of extremely rare birdcage thirty-hour clock by John Ogden of Bowbridge, made with short bob pendulum *c.* 1690 and converted not long after to anchor escapement and long pendulum. Notice the unique square-section posts with square-section caps and bases; these were apparently cast in this shape as cast marks can be seen, for instance at the top of the right-hand pillar.

Plate 90 (*opposite below*). Eight-and-a-half-inch dialsheet, chapter ring, and original single hand of a thirty-hour longcase clock, *c.* 1690, by John Ogden of Bowbridge, Yorkshire. The method of casting the dialsheet with holes, very much a North-country practice, is clearly visible. The side-mounted solid calendar disc, known locally as a 'Westmorland calendar wheel', is read through the square date-box. This gives the outward appearance of a twenty-four-hour calendar change ring (usualy on southern work), whilst in reality it works on the simpler twelve-hour change principle, thus avoiding the cutting of an extra wheel. This calendar system was quite common on thirty-hour clocks in the north-west.

does bring that ability to recognise something almost without the need for thought. It is an instantaneous reaction of the mind, and much of the pleasure of clocks comes through this first-impression recognition. When you have seen enough clocks of a certain type with their correct period hands, one with the wrong hands stands out a mile—you can recognise it across the street.

Everyone has to begin to acquire that experience somewhere. Some can do this through museums, but personally I find that to travel many miles to see something which is untouchable is a sterile operation. There are a few museums who care about and for their clocks—but not many. Some museum clocks are in deplorably dirty condition. The argument that an uncleaned clock is in 'original' condition just does not hold water. Do people really think they were put out to tarnish and rust before being sold 'originally'?

Whether you see yourself as a 'collector' of the most modest kind or the most ambitious, then you cannot possibly work without the basic facts at your disposal. You must have the appropriate reference books—indeed you should have *all* the serious reference books. Exclude 'coffee table' books if you like, for they will give you little but pretty pictures, though even these can be useful for the illustration content.

As a part-time enthusiast it is going to take you no small time to get to know even a few of the ins and outs of the clock world. Suppose you were a doctor, a solicitor, a teacher or an engineer, and suppose that someone said to you that they were thinking of taking up your profession as an interesting hobby at weekends! Yet this is what doctors, solicitors and candlestick-makers often say about clock collecting. They don't stop to consider that a professional clockman, whether restorer or dealer or both, is handling, valuing, buying and selling clocks all day and every day. If a collector hopes to gather even a smattering of clock knowledge, he must expect to take it seriously, to put in a little effort at learning what he can from the books on the subject.

If you venture abroad to buy a clock with a full cheque book and an empty mind, then you will go as a lamb to the slaughter, and there are hundreds of clock butchers waiting for you with knives ready sharpened. If you decided to study a few basic reference books first—it's too late *afterwards*—and there are some books that you will find enjoyable as well as instructive, and let us suppose for a moment that you bought *all* the basic books in print today, then it might cost you over one hundred pounds. But, if you had fifty pounds' worth, you would have a very good start because you could save a hundred pounds on the first clock you bought: all clocks are expensive today and, if you buy rubbish without recognising it as such, then you're going to have difficulty selling it again. Even the books themselves are an investment and you can probably sell them ten years later for more than you paid for them.

I have set out on the following pages a list of books I would recommend. You will not find recommended any books written a hundred years or more ago. More knowledge of clocks has come to light in the last twenty years than in the previous thousand. Antiquated clock books are a wonderfully interesting field in their own right, superb as a hobby for antiquarian book collectors, but do not expect them to teach you about the clocks you will meet in today's high-powered world. Today clocks are changing hands for hundreds and commonly thousands of pounds, and the expertise needed is much more sophisticated than in the days when leisured gentlemen bought horological antiquities for a few shillings a time.

For essential facts and figures you need *Watchmakers and Clockmakers of the World*, a two-volume dictionary of clockmakers, Volume One written by the late G. H. Baillie, Volume Two by myself. These two volumes contain very brief biographical details of over 70,000 makers. This work is the bible of the trade and you will need to refer to it constantly as a quick check on the dates of known makers. A major new work is currently being prepared by myself, *The Clockmakers of Great Britain*, which will attempt to summarise in one several-volume work all known data on each maker. The first volume, on the seventeenth century, is expected in about a year. It is already assumed that you own this book. You then need my *Country Clocks and their London Origins*, which deals largely with provincial British clocks, and also my *The White Dial Clock*, the only book to deal with clocks with painted dials: you must have these because most clocks you see will be either provincial or painted dial, or both. And you need *The Grandfather Clock* by E. L. Edwardes and *The Longcase Clock* by Eric Bruton.

If your interest is in provincially-made clocks, then you ought to buy every county clock book you can get. These are included in the list on pages 251–2. There are not many county books—some are now out of print or in short supply, but county books are one of the few places where you can learn to distinguish local clockmaking and casemaking styles.

If your interest is in lantern clocks, then you need *Weight-driven Chamber Clocks* by E. L. Edwardes. For skeleton clocks F. B. Royer-Collard's copiously-illustrated *Skeleton Clocks* is essential.

If you are interested in London-made clocks then a copy of *English Domestic Clocks* by Herbert Cescinsky and M. R. Webster is well worth having for its illustration content. *Thomas Tompion* by R. W. Symonds and *The Knibb Family Clockmakers* by R. Lee are both superbly detailed studies, but are difficult to obtain. My advice is that you should get *every* modern book on the subject that you can afford.

Having got your 'library' together, the next thing you need is experience. The usual way to get that is to go out and buy the first clock that takes your fancy, get it home, compare it with your books and probably discover that you have bought a 'wrong un'. It is a painful but effective lesson.

Go out and look at all the clocks you can. Experience alone will teach you how to recognise late Victorian engraving from that of earlier periods. It is so very different that anyone familiar with that difference finds it hard to understand how anyone could fail to recognise it. Yet every day people buy clocks with wrong brass dials because they cannot see that obvious difference —and a book cannot teach you that kind of recognition.

So where do you start? What is it that you are supposed to look for that distinguishes a good clock from a mediocre or poor one? I will try to indicate a few points, but first of all try to follow your own inclinations. You may start the quest with a mind still unspoilt by excessive education. Don't let others ruin your taste by foisting their opinions onto you. The chances are that if you like it, others will too, and that alone must make it a desirable clock and therefore a good investment—provided you have done your homework in checking its authenticity, and bearing in mind too that your taste will gradually mature with experience.

To identify a good clock one must see it in relation to others not only of the same type but of the same *period*. For example, if an eight-day London clock of 1690 has five or even six pillars, there is nothing exceptional in that feature. If a *provincial* clock of 1690 had six pillars that would be unusual, while for a provincial clock of 1820 to have six pillars would really be unusual and probably indicate that there was some special reason for the maker to fit the extra two—such as might be the case for a musical clock, a month clock, or one otherwise of long duration. If it were an 1820 eight-day clock with no special features and *still* had six pillars, then that would be a sign of a truly exceptional maker.

The point is that four pillars are adequate except where exceptionally heavy strain is involved, as with a long duration clock. Early London clocks *usually* have five or six pillars for extra rigidity, even though they would mostly have functioned well enough on four, which was normal in provincial work. The early London makers were if anything over-anxious to supply a good product and the signs of this excess of zeal over what was basically essential add up to 'quality'. However, on early London clocks this 'quality' is taken for granted. A provincial maker working in 1750 or 1820 would increasingly be less likely to exhibit such costly zeal and hence such a late clock exhibiting these 'quality' signs indicates an exceptional maker. So, in period, five or even six pillars have no special significance; out of period they are very significant. One can only come to recognise these exceptions by familiarity with the normal.

Nevertheless there follows a list of features which may be to a greater or lesser degree taken for granted in early high-class work, but may be sufficiently unusual to help point out superior work in later clocks and especially in provincial clocks:

split plates after 1690;
latches after about 1710;
highly decorative pillars, especially with fins, after about 1720;
decorative filing and shaping of bell hammer or hammer springs;
two screws through each spandrel rather than one (but watch for replacement spandrels with the old hole left empty);
repeating work on longcase clocks;
ting-tang or musical work;
automated figures;
micrometer suspension control;
unusual pendulum lengths;
shaped steel fittings where brass might be normal;
numbering of clocks.

More obvious externally visible features are:

multiple subdials indicating, e.g., day of the week by name (as opposed to day of the month by number, which is normal), month of the year by name, the year, times at other places as on a world-time dial principal;
astronomical information;
sunrise or sunset features (as opposed to moonwork, which is common);
long duration of run;
alarmwork (other than on an alarm clock);

weights unusually heavy or unusually light (an eight-day usually runs on weights between 10 lbs and 12 lbs, sometimes 14 lbs, each, while a thirty-hour usually runs on one weight of about 8 lbs to 10 lbs);
brass-cased weights, which may be a pointer to a good clock, or may be replacements.

Birdcage thirty-hour movements are often erroneously believed to be earlier than plated ones. On a North-country clock this might be true, but in fact the birdcage design is mostly an indication of region rather than period.

General rules are fraught with exceptions but it is usually the case that after 1720 an arched dial is considered superior to a similar square one; moonwork is a valued feature; calendar work is so common as to make little or no difference unless of an unusual nature, as in the arch; a dial with a raised chapter ring and applied spandrels is superior to a single-sheet brass dial. With painted dials, the eighteenth-century ones by early makers of white dials (e.g., Osborne and Wilson) are superior to the later type, especially when one reaches the heavily painted Victorian period. And, of course, other things being equal (which they rarely are), an early clock is superior to a later one in terms of collectability and quality.

Some signs of poor workmanship (or perhaps signs of clocksmith work, though it should not be possible to camouflage poor workmanship by calling it clocksmithing) are:

rivets holding spandrels;
rivetted chapter rings as opposed to the normal pillar-and-pin fastening;
wheels solid instead of spoked (unusual);
screwheads visible on dial, which is common to hold dial pillars on later London work.

It should be possible to distinguish the ingenious crudity of clocksmith work from poor workmanship of an uninspired nature by seeking the signs of original thinking or practice in the former and the humdrum stereotyped layout of the latter.

In casework many complicated combinations affect the value, and general rules may be of little help. A study of the Gillow cases in Chapter 10 will give some indication of what case features were (and therefore still are) costly, although a costly and elaborate case may not be one that a collector would personally find desirable, and there is a great charm and appeal in some of the earlier and more primitive oak cases, which some collectors may prefer to costlier mahogany or lacquer.

Very generally, it is true that on early (pre-1750) clocks a walnut case, especially if of finely figured walnut veneer rather than plain solid walnut, outrates oak and usually outrates mahogany too (if only because there was little mahogany this early). One should bear in mind that walnut was less often used in North-country work, and mahogany more so, as it came in through Liverpool. A fine walnut marquetry case outrates any other. After 1750 plain solid walnut, while originally no more costly than oak, probably outrates it in today's valuations.

Mahogany usually outrates oak or plain walnut. A lacquer case is very highly esteemed by certain collectors, though the shoddy condition of a great many puts off a lot of people, and some find them too fancy anyway. Black lacquer is the commonest background colour, followed by green, then red, blue and yellow. Lacquer again was less common in the north, where there was a fashion for blackened and carved oak cases. Many connoisseurs dismiss all carved oak cases as Victorian fakes. Nevertheless, a good carved case is highly rated by those with experience of them. Pine cases are the humblest of all, though the fact that many are riddled with woodworm may put a premium on a good clean example.

Regardless of the rules, we all retain our own individual tastes. Some people are not fond of walnut and much prefer mahogany, but most enthusiasts would take the opposite view. For investment, however, one must find a happy compromise between one's own personal likes and dislikes and those of the wider clock world in general.

It is extremely difficult for an absolute beginner to enter the world of clock buying. A person buying his very first clock is well advised to go to a specialist clock dealer and simply buy the clock he likes best which comes within his price range. Without having acquired sufficient knowledge, it can be risky to dabble in the treacherous world of salerooms and junkshops, antique fairs and fleamarkets. Forget all about 'bargains'. A specialist dealer will charge the going price, but one is less likely to be cheated in so far as he will (one hopes) sell one a genuine clock. Even if the dealer charges too much for a clock, at least if you have bought a genuine clock it will come into its own again one day. If you buy a 'wrong un', as you very likely will if you buy it as an inexperienced victim, then you can say goodbye to your money for the foreseeable future.

I have presupposed that you don't want to buy a 'wrong un'. There are people contrary enough not to mind about the works but who will buy what is termed a furnishing-piece, a polite way of saying 'a dud clock that looks attractive'. Only last week such a clock sold for over £300 in a local sale-room. It had no works at all—just a dial with an electric motor behind.

Let us turn our attention to investment. If you fear that I am about to tell you about someone who bought long-forgotten Tompions out of cellars between the wars for a few shillings a time, then you may be relieved to know that I am not. Such tales, true or otherwise, are infuriating to an enthusiast who was probably not even born at the time, and they are irrelevant to today's situation.

'But will it be an investment?' is the question that almost every clock-buyer asks. If one were able to see into the future, one could provide the answer. Instead, the best that one can do is to look back over the last few years to see what has happened. (Any values are exact at the time of writing, 1977.)

In 1967 I bought my first clock specifically intending to resell it. It was an eight-day provincial square brass dial in an oak longcase—ordinary, but two hundred years old and good. There was no question of cleaning or restoring it. It ran well enough on a two-hundred-year accumulation of grime and a spot of oil. It sold for £35 (about $100) to dealers from Holland. Today that same clock would sell for about £700 (about $1,300) to a trade buyer.

Can it go on like that? Exactly the same question was asked in 1967 when I offered that £35 clock for sale. But it has gone on, and it shows no signs of stopping. Quite the reverse. That £700 clock would have cost only half as much as recently as 1975.

In an inflationary society antique clocks are all free, anyway. All that clock dealers do is to act as a free lending library for clocks. They raise the initial investment capital, find the goods, put them in order, and then lend them free to the customer for as long as he likes. After a couple of years or more, if he gets tired of them, the clock dealer will buy them back again, certainly for no less than they cost the customer initially, and probably giving him interest on his investment. So, if you want a clock, or a houseful—have them, they're all free!

Before we get further into values and investment percentages, let me make one point. All along I am referring to 'right' clocks, clocks that are not faked or butchered or 'converted' or otherwise spoiled—which immediately rules out six out of every ten clocks that one comes across, for a great many are duds. (Just yesterday a local saleroom offered six longcase clocks, and all six were glaringly wrong: the top price reached was £1,500 (about $3,000).) However, if you do buy a 'wrong' clock and then find you cannot sell it at all, you are on your own and you have only yourself to blame. It follows that, unless you are already a clock expert, you should buy from recognised clock dealers, who may charge you for the privilege but are less likely to sell you wrong goods.

Let's recap a little and look at that appreciation scale again. Remember, we are talking of ordinary provincial clockwork—excluding special makers, special types of clock and special features.

	1967	1974–5	1977
8-day square brass dial c. 1770	£35	£350	£700
8-day arched painted dial c. 1820	£12	£200	£400
30-hour brass dial c. 1770	£20	£250	£500
30-hour painted dial c. 1800	£8	£125	£250

These are approximate figures. The period of the clocks was not terribly important because painted dial clocks were all lumped together, whether made in 1775 or 1840, and the same was true with thirty-hour brass dials, whether 1690 or 1790. In 1967 few people made any distinction in 'quality' (except for the obviously very famous names) although a pretty case would bring more than a scruffy one, and London on the dial meant that everyone instantly recognised it as a desirable item, whether it was or not. In fact in 1967 few could tell a 1770 white dial from an 1840 one.

The whole point was that, with values so low, it did not matter. Today it is very different. The 1977 figures in the table are therefore very approximate because the individual qualities of a clock have a much greater bearing on the price. While we show £400 for an eight-day white dial, the price could be as high as £700 or more and, if it were exceptional, there would be no limit.

The rule used to be that London clocks were fine, provincial ones were no good. If you had to buy provincial clocks, then thirty-hours were a waste of time and everyone knew that painted dial clocks were made in factories. Fortunately we have learned something about our clock heritage since then, and by 'then' we are only talking of less than twenty years ago. The understanding of clocks is a new sphere. We are at the dawn of a new age of appreciation. It is only just beginning and there is still plenty of time to enter, even for a complete beginner. If you had been a clock enthusiast in 1950, then most of the historical information, guides and recognition aspects detailed earlier in this book, and now accepted as fact, would not have been available to you. Collecting British clocks, in a general sense, is a new science, a young pursuit.

Clock prices have just about doubled over the last two to three years. One does not imagine that this rapid pace will continue, but even looking at appreciation values between 1967 and 1974, where progress was more gradual, we have seen at least a tenfold price rise.

Suppose, therefore, you bought our £35 example in 1967, and for argument's sake let us imagine that you were swindled, and paid the extortionate price then of £100—three times the clock's actual worth. Don't worry. You could not have got your money back for a year or two, but by 1974 you could, with a good surplus (totally free of tax, remember); and by 1977 you could look back with pride at what a good buy you had only ten years ago—always provided that you bought 'right' goods—despite inflation.

The moral is that it is *what* you buy that matters most and not the price you pay for it. Your first task is therefore to leave junk to junk dealers. If you are buying honest clocks, forget the price. If ever the clock market takes a tumble, the first thing that the bottom will drop out of is the rubbish market. If you have honest clocks, people will want to buy them. If you have good clocks, so much the better. People will be fighting each other to buy them from you.

So far we have talked about typical longcase clocks, if one can suppose that any of them are 'typical' in that sense. However, if you had been armed with foresight in 1967, you could have predicted that some types would increase in value more than others, and thus have indulged in judicial selection. Thirty-hour brass dial clocks were underrated and so were white dial clocks of all types—largely because of the influence of misguided books of half a century ago which taught that eight-day brass dials were the only sort worth having. If you had bought (without real knowledge, even) in those categories, the chances are that you had a better investment than in straightforward eight-day brass dials. It should be pointed out, however, that eight-day brass dials still have the highest single demand and therefore your potential selling market would be larger.

If, in 1967, you had the ability to buy selectively by exercising your own skills in identifying better-quality work, then the likelihood is that you made a better investment still. Because what must surely happen as prices continue to rise is that the price-range of certain types of clock will spread, so that better goods fetch very much higher prices than mediocre work. This was not so in 1967, when an overseas buyer could order them by the dozen, unseen, at a standard unit price, with no regard to the 'quality' of the individual item, and frequently without regard to whether the clocks were 'right' or 'wrong'.

What you buy must depend on the amount of money you have to spend. If you want to collect clocks at £10,000 or £20,000 apiece, then obviously you need a different approach from the man who has a matter of hundreds to spend. A year ago at a saleroom my wife happened to be standing next to someone who had just bought his first two clocks (they were bracket clocks) in the sale at a total outlay of £9,500 (about $18,500). He did not even know how to carry the two clocks, which every dealer in the room knew were 'wrong'. The dealer who had put the clocks in the sale was of course delighted, and dashed off home to make some more clocks for the next victim.

My suggestion is that such a buyer should go to a dealer who specialises in that costly type of clock and put himself in his hands for guidance. All you have to do at any time to test the good faith of any dealer, large or small, is to try selling a clock back to him and see what response you get. So, if you want to buy Tompions and the like, remember that this very specialised market is excluded from the remarks which follow.

If you are a more down-to-earth buyer with a limited amount to spend, in which direction might you best channel it from the investment point of view? Remember a more purist 'collector' may not be interested primarily in investment but more in aesthetics, and therefore will himself know in which direction he should go. There are several categories of clock which seem to me to be undervalued relative to others. Looking first at brass dial clocks, one ought to be able to select those of best quality, whether by makers who are just beginning to be recognised—e.g., Thomas Ogden, Henry Hindley and the like—or by unknown makers who are as yet unrecognised for the merit which their clocks nevertheless have. Then there is the largely untapped field of thirty-hour clocks, where some of the early ones can be very exciting (e.g., the John Greenbanck shown in plate 22) and vastly superior to mediocre late examples; the price difference may not necessarily represent the full potential of that difference—as yet.

Coming to painted dials, I think there is much more merit in some of the late eighteenth-century ones (say, 1775–1800) than is reflected in their cost as compared with, for example, a brass dial equivalent from that time—although I doubt whether traditional opinions will ever fade to the point where the two types are treated as equal. The 1775–1800 ones are generally better than the 1800–1830 ones, which are likewise better than the 1830–1870 ones, yet prices do not always distinguish this difference adequately. Thirty-hour painted dials seem to me to be especially neglected, and yet eighteenth-century examples can be most interesting clocks. This distinction in period applies especially to, for example, English wall dial clocks, where a Victorian one may look superficially like a late eighteenth-century one, and yet there is a considerable difference in the true worth of each which the price may not truly reflect.

Any type of clock which has rare or unusual or desirable extra features must be one to select for investment. A cuckoo clock (these are not British-made, of course) with a bird popping out every hour might be considered ordinary; one where a hunter pops out and shoots the bird would be unusual; one of the latter made by Thomas Tompion, and you can name your own price!

On longcase clocks, the casework is a very important factor, perhaps inordinately so, since the case may be responsible for the clock's finding a buyer or not. Indeed, it is not unknown for people to buy a clock solely on account of the attractiveness of the case and with no regard at all to the clock it houses. This is a pity but nevertheless has to be taken into account when considering investment, since one's investment is only as good as the potential demand when one comes to selling. The bigger the demand the better the investment will prove, and unfortunately this applies even if the high-demand market is an ignorant one. The best purchase for the investor must therefore be that which is 'right', interesting horologically, and in a pretty case, ideally the original case—thereby appealing to all possible sectors of the market.

Because many longcase movements have been re-housed over the years in other cases, there are now three types of combinations: those where one can be quite certain that the case is original, those where one can be certain they are in the wrong cases, and those where the cases could well be right but one just cannot know for sure—the latter group forming the majority.

If one can be sure the case is right, these clocks should be at the very top of their range. If the case is wrong, then obviously there has to be some-thing very special about the clock to make it desirable. As for the majority, if the case is 'right' in period, character and regional style, then I think one has to accept it as a valid case for the clock, whether or not the clock began its life with that actual case. Views differ greatly about the question of case-swapping. The discerning collector buying a clock for himself probably would not want to live with it unless he could feel certain it had its original case—with the possible exception of a clock which had some very special attraction for him.

Many of the above investment tips may simply reflect the difference between the good and the mediocre and may well include the same kind of aspects which a collector looks for in his search for clocks of interest or quality—though not necessarily so, for the collector tends to seek what he personally sees as having merit, while an investor seeks only those merits which he hopes will later be widely appreciated financially.

Ideally, one hopes that the collecting and investing elements will be balanced within the same person, for it is sad to think of business houses, investment groups and financiers dabbling in clocks in the same way that they might with shares and commodities.

The ordinary purchaser of a clock buys it because he likes it and hopes to get pleasure from owning it and caring for it. Investment is not the main consideration in his mind, but it is still there at the *back* of his mind. He finds reassurance in the knowledge that, if bad times come and he is pressed for funds, it should be possible to sell the clock again without losing, and ideally with a certain appreciation on what may have represented to him a very significant capital outlay. He can take comfort in the fact that, provided he exercises a little common sense when buying, the purchase of a clock should fulfil his expectations in terms of investment.

12 Outstanding Makers
and Outstanding Work

*. . . to my cousin . . . two pieces of clockwork, one of them being in the fform
of a cuckow and the other in the fform of a Milk Maid . . .*

(Bequest from the will of Daniel
Winnock of London, clockmaker, died
1726, grandson of Ahasuerus Fromanteel.)

———————◆———————

The cost of clocks—some examples, ordinary and extraordinary—Clock Clubs—
runaway apprentices—one who changed his name—checklist of names, famous
and unknown

Most clockmakers, especially provincial ones, made their livelihoods by
producing sturdy and reliable clocks of a relatively standardised type. To
the enthusiast, the occasional maker who displayed originality of thought
gives that little sparkle to a quest that could easily become a mundane
examination of stereotyped features. I suppose every maker must have
allowed himself an occasional wild fling at creating something above the
level of his ordinary product, whether for his own personal satisfaction or
use, or for a very wealthy customer.

It was, of course, money which determined what a clockmaker produced,
because a clock was usually the most costly single item in any household,
and it was not an easy task to get money out of even those customers who
had plenty. Wealthy gentry seem to have thought nothing of taking three or
four years to settle their accounts, a problem which may have been more
serious in Scotland, as this advertisement from the *Aberdeen Journal* of 1753
suggests:

216

Hugh Gordon, watchmaker, begs . . . to acquaint . . . that since his settle-ment in Aberdeen [from Edinburgh and London] he has lost a much greater sum than can be easily believed, by people neglecting to pay for the cleaning and repairing of their clocks and watches, which at last forced him, much against his inclination, to acquaint his employers in this public manner that for the future he is to clean and mend for *ready money only* . . .

If we exclude the case, then in the eighteenth century the average price was about £2.10.0 (£2.50) for a thirty-hour brass-dial clock and about £4.00.00 for an eight-day. These prices did not change very much over the years, because inflation was balanced by the economies of increasing specialisation. They would have applied more or less equally in 1800 as in 1700.

Of course, a very famous maker could charge whatever he liked. Thomas Tompion, for instance, in the late seventeenth century, is known to have charged £6.00.00. for a common thirty-hour clock in a black (ebonised pine) case—about twice the normal price. For a walnut-cased month longcase he charged £25.00.00. For a spring (bracket) clock and stand (bracket) he charged £31.10.0 (£31.50); for a tortoiseshell spring clock £40.00.00; and for an ebony repeating quarter-chiming spring clock £75–£95.

Here is an interesting pricelist of work by clockmaker Job Rider of Belfast dating from the late 1780s:

	£	s.	d.
A seven-tune chime with springs	22.	5.	7.
ditto with weights	19.	4.	9.
,, 3-stop organ	25.	11.	10.
Made upon Harrison's construction with a pendulum which is not affected by heat or cold	11.	7.	6.
Another kind inferior	10.	4.	9.
Moon common, without case (i.e., 8-day)	5.	13.	9.
Square (dial) ditto ditto (i.e., without case)	5.	0.	0.

NB Various other clocks made according to order upon the lowest terms.
(Notes in brackets by author)

There is one example of a top maker setting his own price, which I cannot resist quoting, because this instance puts into the shadows such a 'famous' maker as Joseph Knibb alongside a true genius such as Fromanteel. A certain Mercator, a gifted German mathematician, had engaged Ahasuerus Froman-teel to make a clock of a complex nature to show the equation of time. Mercator then presented to King Charles II this (?bracket) clock: '(twas of a

Plate 91. Early japanned dial from a clock by Thomas Solomon of Penzance, made about 1785. Solomon died in 1793.

foote diameter), which shewed the inequality of the sunn's motion from the apparent motion, which the King did understand by his informations, and did commend it, but he never had a penny of him for it. This curious clock was neglected, and somebody of the court happened to become master of it, who understood it not; he sold it to Mr. Knib, a watchmaker, who did not understand it neither, who sold it to Mr. Fromantle (that made it) for £5, who askes now [1683] for it £200.'

This little incident seems to sum up very neatly the Royal interest in the Royal toys. A masterpiece, paid for by an ingratiator, made by a dedicated genius, was played with, put aside until forgotten and finally sold off as junk by some court hanger-on. What is even more surprising is that an eminent maker such as Joseph Knibb, himself a man of great talent and originality of thought, could not make head or tail of it. It must have taken years for Knibb to live down the embarrassment of this incident; he was nevertheless

Plate 92. Dial of the thirty-hour clock by John Woolley of Codnor, *c.* 1775. Though only a Cottage Clock the workmanship is of the highest calibre. The spandrels are well-finished, detailed and clean of all casting rag. The engraving is deeply and boldly cut, artistically pleasing and clearly legible. Excellent country work.

one of the finest clockmakers of all time. Once back in the hands of the maker, however, the clock instantly regained its true significance and worth.

Unusual clocks, even by makers who were not famous, naturally cost more money. A musical clock was a very costly item in the eighteenth century. One fashion was to have a clock that each hour (or sometimes every third or fourth hour) played a different tune for each day of the week, and a hymn on Sundays. These usually played on eight bells, but some did so on ten or twelve, occasionally on many more. William Porthouse of Penrith quoted a price of eleven guineas to make such a clock in 1784—that would be without the case. In 1741 Thomas Moore of Ipswich supplied an eight-day quarter-chiming clock in a walnut case at £16.16.0. (£16.80).

Special clockwork of a complex nature has always been very expensive. In 1794 the widow of William Downie, an Edinburgh clockmaker, tried to sell a complicated musical clock: 'It has dead seconds from the centre, moon's age and a tide table. It chimes 9 tunes upon 18 bells and is in the most perfect order, having been only set agoing within these few months and was valued by Mr. Downie himself at *forty guineas* . . .' The *Edinburgh Evening Courant* of 1785 gives another example:

> James Gray of Edinburgh . . . after great labour and much expense . . . has finished a most elegant musical clock . . . The clock goes eight days, and plays a tune of itself three times over every three hours in the day. It plays 10 different tunes, which may be shifted at pleasure by turning a hand on the dial. While the music plays two figures dance, and a musician plays on the violin, all of them keeping accurate time to the music. There is likewise represented a landscape and rural scene, with a windmill going, and a number of figures of various character walking along in regular procession. As also a distant view of an encampment, with a soldier on duty constantly walking backward and forward, and may be seen at no. 19, Princes Street . . . to be sold by lottery, but valued at eighty guineas.

It seems that clockmakers who made such automata did not find it easy to sell them, and they were not infrequently offered by lottery. This shortage of ready money was no doubt the reason why N. MacPherson of Edinburgh hired out clocks and watches 'by the month or year'. Another way round the money problem was the Clock Club. George Munro announced in the *Caledonian Mercury* in 1764: 'He intends to begin a clock and watch club about the end of the month. Those that want a clock or watch in that way may send their names betwixt and that time.' This was an early type of hire-purchase system. If a clock cost fifty shillings, then the club had fifty members each paying one shilling per week (or month), or perhaps twenty-five members paying two shillings. Each week one member, selected by drawing lots, got his clock, for which the clockmaker got his full money. The difficulty was that the other members had to ensure that those who got the goods after only one or two payments, kept on paying until the full fifty shillings was paid up by each person. Quite a number of clockmakers are known to have run clock clubs. George Munro's must have been a success for in 1777 he ran a Gold Watch Club.

It was hard enough getting money out of the customers, but to make matters worse if the clockmaker turned his back his own workmen often ran off with his stock. The *Edinburgh Gazette* of 1699 gives one example:

James Barrow, aged about twenty, of a low stature, a little pock-marked, speaks the English accent, had on when he went away a short flaxen coll cut wig, in an ordinary habit, run away from his master [Andrew Brown of Edinburgh] the nineteenth instant, with a plain gold watch without a christal, with an enambiled dial, the emembling on the figures is broken off, a silver pendulum watch with a minute hand made by W. Young at Charing Cross, London . . . whoever can secure the said youth and give notice thereof to Captain Andrew Brown, watchmaker in Edinburgh, shall have two guineas reward.

Another instance, from the *Edinburgh Evening Courant* of 1792, describes how

Wm. Muir, an Englishman journeyman Clockmaker with Mr. John Russell, Falkirk, went off on Monday, 25th, carrying away eight silver watches . . . He appears to be a man between 30 and 40 years of age, about five feet five inches high, short black hair, thin on the forehead, a large mark of a cut upon the right corner of his brow; had on when he went off a snuff brown coat tore at the right armpit, dark brown velveret vest with small yellow spots, plain drab-coloured breeches, round hat, blue-white stockings, and shoes tied with leather thongs . . .

There were plenty of these runaway apprentices and journeymen, many of them heavily laden with the master's stock. A journeyman, by the nature of his employment, was one who worked as a helper under a master, moving as the occasion needed from one master to another. There were many thousands of makers who worked in this way, and therefore clocks or watches made by them are unknown because they worked anonymously; just occasionally, their names are found hidden away inside clock movements. With this anonymity, it must have been possible for many a runaway to move a few hundred miles off and start afresh with a new master—and a man could change his name easily enough if he wished, as no doubt many runaways did. There is the interesting story of one Thomas Norweb, whose widow ended her days in the workhouse in Brigg in Lincolnshire, where in 1812 she wrote her memoirs entitled *The Memoirs of Janetta: a tale, alas, too true*. She describes how, after a gay life in London, she was banished to Richmond, Yorkshire, where she met a schoolmaster, Thomas Norweb, who had been trained initially as a watchmaker. Why he changed trades we do not know. They married in Scotland and moved to Wetherby, Yorkshire, where a child was born in 1766 and where the father took up his old watchmaking trade again, but went bankrupt. He moved to practise the trade at Selby, where another child was born in 1769, then to Brigg, where he spent twelve years as a silversmith. Then he had four years as a clockmaker at Louth, first as a journeyman, then on his own. He died in Brigg workhouse in 1809. His widow died there in 1817 aged 77. This is not just a sad story, but also an intriguing one. The name Norweb does not exist; it is an invented name, apparently originating in 1766 at Richmond, and it happens to be an anagram of Browne. Was Thomas Norweb or Browne a runaway? It looks rather that way.

It is interesting to reflect that at this time the rates of pay for journeymen clockmakers were very low. In 1655 William Rogers' journeyman, Abraham Vanacker, was paid five shillings weekly, rising to six shillings later. On the other hand, this rate might be a little lower than average, as the native clockmakers could often get 'alien' workers at a cheap rate, which was one very good reason why they employed them whenever they could get away with it.

The folklore, customs, history, all these are part and parcel of the clock enthusiast's interest in his subject, but the real interest of beginner or expert, is to find unappreciated and undervalued treasures. To help those innocent enough to believe that this is still possible, and as a quick checklist for the rest of us, there follows a series of names.

The list below contains brief details of the best-known London makers, some of them very famous. Many London makers played a prominent part in the running of the Clockmakers' Company and in due course held the senior positions of Assistant, Warden and ultimately of Master. These offices were all attainable *on length of service* by active members and it is quite misleading to believe that the holding of the office of Master implied a special honour done to a member as a reward for excellence at the craft, an impression that is sometimes given. Those early makers who became Master on more than one occasion did so because they managed to manipulate the holding of the offices, and this is not a sign that they were *ipso facto* especially eminent clockmakers.

Langley BRADLEY. Apprenticed 1687 to Joseph Wise. Clockmakers' Company member 1695–1738. Worked at the Minute Dial in Fenchurch Street. Known for longcase and bracket clocks, but especially for turret clocks, particularly that made for St. Paul's in 1708.

William CLEMENT. Apprenticed 1657 to Thomas Chapman in the Blacksmiths' Company, where he became a freeman in 1665. Did not join the Clockmakers' Company till 1677. Worked near to Fromanteel in Southwark, where he died in 1704. Known for turret clocks and longcase clocks and is often credited with the invention of the anchor escapement.

Daniel DELANDER. Apprenticed 1692 to Charles Halstead. Clockmakers' Company member from 1699 until his death in 1733. Known for longcase and bracket clocks and watches.

Edward EAST. Born 1602, apprenticed to Richard Rogers in the Goldsmiths' Company, where he was a freeman in 1627. Very famous for watches and to a lesser extent for clocks. Worked in Fleet Street and was a very influential figure throughout his long life. In 1660 was appointed Chief Clockmaker to the King, an office he held until his death in 1696 aged 94.

John EBSWORTH. Apprenticed 1657 to Richard Aymes, Clockmakers' Company freeman 1665 until his death in 1699. Worked at the Cross Keys in Lothbury. Known through lantern, longcase and bracket clocks and watches.

Ahasuerus FROMANTEEL the elder. Born 1607 in Norwich. Went to London 1629. Died 1693. The most important British clockmaker of all time. Introduced the pendulum to Britain in 1658. Worked at Mosses Alley, Southwark.

Ahasuerus FROMANTEEL, junior, and John FROMANTEEL. Sons of Ahasuerus senior. Worked with him and then transferred the family business to Amsterdam about 1680.

Christopher GOULD. Entered the Clockmakers' Company in 1682 as a turret clock maker, though he is also famous for longcase and bracket clocks and watches. Worked 'near the north-east corner of the Royal Exchange'. Died 1718.

George GRAHAM. Born 1673, apprenticed 1688 to Henry Aske. Partner of and successor to Tompion after his death in 1713. Credited with the invention of the cylinder escapement for watches. Best known for watches; his clocks are not commonly met with.

Charles GRETTON. Apprenticed 1662 to Humphrey Downing. Member of the Clockmakers' Company 1672 to 1733. Known for longcase clocks and watches.

Henry JONES. Apprenticed 1654 to Edward East. Freeman of the Clockmakers' Company 1663 to his death in 1695. Very famous maker who worked 'in the Temple'. Known through longcase and bracket clocks and watches.

John KNIBB. Born 1650. Worked with brother, Joseph, at Oxford. Died 1722.

Joseph KNIBB. Born 1640. Working in Oxford by 1665, moved to London in 1670. Retired to Buckinghamshire in 1697, where he died in 1711. A very famous maker of great originality.

Samuel KNIBB. Father of John and Joseph Knibb. Came from Newport Pagnell to London and entered the Clockmakers' Company in 1663; died before 1674. A fine maker whose very rare clocks seem to be based closely on Fromanteel designs.

Thomas LOOMES. Working from 1649 to his death about 1665. Succeeded John Selwood at the Mermaid in Lothbury in 1651. His work is known only through a few lantern clocks. From 1658 he was in partnership with Ahasuerus Fromanteel the elder and his fame arises purely out of this partnership.

Thomas MUDGE. Born 1715, died 1794. Entered the Clockmakers' Company in 1738. Succeeded George Graham in Fleet Street. Famed for his work in precision timekeeping, especially in watches and chronometers.

Daniel QUARE. A very famous maker who worked in Exchange Alley. Born 1649. Entered the Clockmakers' Company in 1671 as a maker of turret clocks.

After 1718 he was in partnership with Stephen Horseman until his death in 1724. Known through longcase and bracket clocks and watches.

Robert SEIGNIOR. Apprenticed to John Nicasius until 1667 when he became a freeman of the Clockmakers' Company working in Exchange Alley, but also had connections with York. In 1674 he was appointed Clock and Watch Maker to the King to succeed Edward East when the latter retired or died. In fact East lived to such a ripe age that Seignior died first, in 1687. Known through longcase and bracket clocks and watches.

Edward STAUNTON. Apprenticed in 1655 to Nathaniel Allen. Made a freeman of the Clockmakers' Company in 1662. Worked in Leadenhall Street until about 1707. Known through longcase clocks and watches.

Thomas TOMPION. Born 1639, died 1713. Probably the most famous clock-maker of all time. Made clocks but mostly watches from his arrival in London about 1671, where he worked at the Dial and Three Crowns in Water Lane. Briefly in partnership with Edward Banger about 1701 to 1708, then with George Graham (about 1711 to 1713) who succeeded him.

Joseph WILLIAMSON. Trained in Ireland before entering the Clockmakers' Company as a turret clock maker in 1686. Died 1725. Known for longcase clocks.

Joseph WINDMILLS. Entered the Clockmakers' Company as a turret clock maker in 1671. Worked initially 'at St. Martins Le Grand', later in Tower Street with his son, Thomas, until about 1723. Known for lantern and longcase clocks.

Here follows a list of provincial makers whose work, usually in eight-day clocks, is known to me personally to be often above average, but whose clocks as yet may not command the prices they merit. There must naturally be many others whose work is not known to me. All are known for longcase clocks unless otherwise stated.

William BELLMAN of Broughton (Lancashire). Working 1790–c. 1812.

John BENSON of Whitehaven. Working from *c.* 1750, died 1798.

Nathaniel BROWN of Manchester. Working *c.* 1760–*c.* 1770.

John BURGESS of Wigan. Married 1711, died 1754.

Emanuel BURTON of Kendal. Three of this name in succession from about 1720 to 1830.

John CLIFTON of Liverpool. Working from 1777 until his death in 1794.

The COATES family of Wigan. Archibald I, working from 1759, died 1797. His sons, Archibald II, Robert and James succeeded him until about 1800.

Edward COCKEY of Warminster. Working *c.* 1750 until *c.* 1780.

Thomas CROFTS of Halton (Leeds). Working 1752–1756.

Thomas CRUTTENDEN. Born 1657, apprenticed in London to Robert Seignior. Freeman of the Clockmakers' Company in 1677, free at York 1679, where he worked till his death in 1698. Lantern and longcase clocks known.

Barnaby DAMMANT of Colchester. Born 1683, died 1738.

Samuel DEACON of Barton (Leicestershire). Born 1746, died 1816.

William DRURY of Gainsborough. Working *c.* 1730 until *c.* 1740.

Abraham FARRER of Pontefract. Working *c.* 1695 until his death in 1754.

Peter FEARNLEY of Wigan. Married 1776, died 1826.

The FINNEYS of Liverpool. John: 1761–1795; Joseph I: born about 1708, died 1772; Joseph II, fl. 1790.

Isaac HADWEN of Liverpool. Born 1723, died 1767.

George HALIFAX of Doncaster. Born 1725, died 1811.

John HALIFAX of Barnsley. Born 1695, working 1718, died 1750.

Joseph HALIFAX of Barnsley. Born 1728, died 1762.

Thomas HALIFAX of Barnsley. Born 1721. Later went to London, where he died in 1789.

Ambrose HAWKINS of Exeter. Working from 1695, died 1705.

Robert HENDERSON of Scarborough. Born 1678, working around 1700, died 1756.

Henry HINDLEY of Wigan. Born 1701, moved to York by 1730, died 1771.

William HOLLOWAY of Stroud. Working 1666 until *c.* 1685, died 1695.

Emanuel HOPPERTON of Leeds. Born 1705, died 1753.

Thomas HUSBAND of Hull. Working around 1760, died 1812.

Anthony HUTCHINSON of Leeds. Working *c.* 1745 until *c.* 1780.

Jonathan LEES of Bury. Working *c.* 1730, died 1785.

Thomas LISTER junior of Halifax. Born 1745, died 1814.

James LOMAX of Blackburn. Born 1749, died 1814.

Hugh LOUGH of Penrith. Working about 1760, died 1790.

Morgan LOWRY of Leeds. Born 1682, married 1703, died 1757.

Richard MIDGELEY of Halifax. Working *c.* 1740–*c.* 1763.

Thomas MOORE of Ipswich. Working *c.* 1740–*c.* 1756.

Joseph MORTON of Aberford. Born *c.* 1720, died 1774.

James and William NEWBY of Kendal. Working *c.* 1760–*c.* 1800.

William NICHOLSON of Whitehaven. Working *c.* 1735–*c.* 1765.

Isaac NICKOLS of Wells. fl. 1740 (maybe from London, *c.* 1700).

Thomas OGDEN of Halifax. Famous Quaker clockmaker. Born 1693, married 1724, died 1769.

Henry PHILIPSON senior. Born 1754 Winster. To Ulverston about 1805, where he died 1834.

Thomas RADFORD of Leeds. Born 1731, married 1759, died 1801.

Dollif ROLLISON, senior and junior of Halton (Leeds). The father worked from *c.* 1720, died 1752. The son born 1752, moved to Sheffield by 1779, working there until about 1790.

Ralph ROWNTREE of York. Born 1673, married 1696.

Robert ROWNTREE of York. Working 1822–1834.

John SMALLWOOD of Chelford/Macclesfield. fl. 1710, died 1715.

Jeremiah STANDRING of Bolton. Born 1712, married 1742, died, 1782.

William TIPLING of Leeds. Married 1692, died 1712.

John WILLIAMSON. London 1682, to Leeds 1683, died 1748.

John WILSON of Peterborough. 1757–1795.

Here follows a list of provincial makers of humbler clocks, many of them of the clocksmith type. Clocks by these makers are usually much better in quality than run-of-the-mill work.

Jonas BARBER senior. Born 1688 at Skipton, working at Bowland Bridge, Westmorland, by 1717, then at Winster by 1727. Died 1764.

Jonas BARBER junior of Winster. Born about 1718, died 1802.

Christopher CAYGILL of Askrigg. Born 1747, married 1769, died 1803.

Aaron CHEESEBROUGH of Penrith. Working about 1690, died 1749.

Abel COTTEY. Born 1655 at Crediton. Went to Philadelphia 1682 where he died in 1711.

Robert DAVIS of Burnley. Working 1723.

John GREEN of Skipton. Working 1704, died 1742.

John GREENBANCK, place unknown. fl. 1690.

Isaac HADWEN. Born 1687. Worked at Kendal and Sedbergh. Died 1737 on a visit to USA.

Thomas LISTER senior of Luddenden (near Halifax). Born 1717, working 1738, died 1779.

John OGDEN of Askrigg. Born about 1660 at Halifax. To Askrigg c. 1680, died 1741.

Samuel OGDEN of Halifax. Born 1669. working there until 1727, then to Benwell (Newcastle-upon-Tyne).

William PORTHOUSE of Penrith. Born 1706, died 1790.

(William?) POWLEY of Asby (Westmorland). Working about 1750, believed died 1768.

Benoni PULLAN of Bradford. Born 1697, married 1725, died 1750.

Samuel ROPER of Crewkerne. Born 1707, died 1759.

John SHEPLEY, probably of Stockport. Working from c. 1700, died 1750.

Robert SKELTON of Malton. Working *c.* 1760–*c.* 1790.

William SNOW senior of Padside. Born 1736, married 1765, died 1795.

John STANCLIFFE of Halifax. Born 1706, died 1780.

Joseph STANCLIFFE of Halifax. Born 1740, died 1812.

Joshua STANCLIFFE of Halifax. Born 1708, died *c.* 1770.

Batty STORR of York. Born 1710, died 1793.

Jonathan STORR of York. Born 1739, died 1805.

William TROUTBECK of Leeds. Married 1709, died 1738.

Robert WATTS of Stamford. Working 1757–1759.

Edward WEBB of Chewstoke. Working 1688–1693. Lantern clocks.

James WHITTAKER of Middleton (Manchester). Working *c.* 1700, died 1720.

James WOOLLEY of Codnor (Derbyshire). Born *c.* 1700, died 1786.

John WOOLLEY of Codnor (Derbyshire). Born 1738, died 1795.

Glossary

Anchor escapement: The anchor is the name given to the shaped steel double-edged lever which allows the escape wheel to turn as it rocks from side to side. The shaped points of contact with the escape wheel teeth are called pallets. (See figure 14). Invention of the anchor escapement in the 1660s has been credited to several people but remains uncertain. As the angle of swing of an anchor escapement pendulum is much less than with the older verge escapement, this permitted a longer pendulum to be used, thereby enforcing a more accurate control on the timekeeping.

Arbor: A steel axle to which a wheel is attached at one end and a pinion at the other, generally pivoted between the clock plates. Also applied to any pivoted rotating steel shaft in clockwork.

Balance wheel: The earliest British form of clock regulator, being a single-spoked wheel of iron rotating back and forth on an upright staff (called a verge), impelled by the teeth of the escape wheel which push alternately against projections on the staff. Its function was to slow down the speed of the clock to a regular pace. It was found on the earliest lantern clocks and spring-driven table clocks but was superceded by the pendulum *c.* 1658 as a more accurately controllable regulator. (See figure 1.)

Fig. 14. The anchor escapement. This typical anchor escapement shows the shape of the teeth of the escape wheel and the shaped pallets of the anchor itself.

Fig. 15. Arbor with seven-leaved pinion cut from the solid and with no collet. The wheel was mounted onto the square filed shank. This arbor is from a lantern clock, c1670, by Edward Norris of London.

Fig. 16. Some typical examples of brass wheel collets showing variations in style relative to period. Numbers *1*, *2* and *3* date from the early to middle eighteenth century; *4*, *5* and *6* are from the late eighteenth century; and *7* and *8* are early nineteenth-century examples. Each maker would vary the style according to his own design. *9* is a very early example, being an all-steel pinion with integral collet turned from the solid, taken from the clock, c1685, by William Holloway of Stroud shown in Plate 36: notice the tapered arbor, a feature found on many early clocks. *10* is from a clock by James Whittaker of Middleton, Lancashire, c. 1690, again a tapered arbor. *11* is from a clock by Quare of London, also c. 1690, and has a parallel arbor; *12* is a simplified London collet of c. 1720 while *13* shows the more decorative and superior work of a provincial maker of the same period, John Green of Skipton. All except *9* are brass collets driven onto the arbors.

232

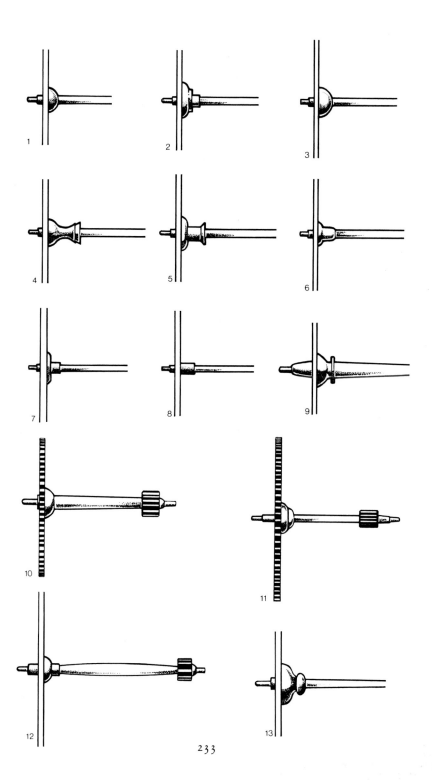

Barrel: Hollow brass drum attached to the winding arbor and carrying the weight-line, being allowed to wind (but not to unwind) by means of a ratchet and click. On spring-driven clocks the spring is contained within the barrel.

Birdcage: The normal term used to describe the layout of a thirty-hour posted or post-framed movement, differing from a plate movement in having upright posts (as against horizontal pillars) by which to hold the top and base plates together. In birdcage movements the clock trains lie one behind the other, while in plated movements they lie side by side. It was ultimately superseded everywhere by the plated form of thirty-hour construction. (See plate 60.)

Bolt and shutter: See Maintaining power.

Centre-seconds: A long seconds-hand concentric with hour and minute hands on a longcase clock, often used together with a centre calendar. Such a clock normally has a dead-beat escapement, *q.v.*

Chapter ring: Brass ring on a clock dial on which the numbers are engraved. Usually refers to the hours and minutes ring but also used for seconds, calendar, strike/silent work, musical selection feature, etc. In these latter instances it is usual to specify which ring is meant.

Collet: A boss or boss-shaped washer fulfilling two different functions and best identified as either a hands collet (a domed brass washer which holds the minute hand in position by means of a pin to keep the tension correct) or a wheel collet (a small brass washer-like disc used to attach a wheel to an arbor). The collet is soldered or brazed or just friction-fitted to the arbor, then the wheel to the collet. The shapes of wheel collets can act as a guide to age and of course one oddly shaped collet in a train of wheels can indicate a replaced wheel. Early collets are usually more elaborately turned than later ones which ultimately become a mere cylindrical shape. Gentler, rounded shapes tend to be earlier than more severe ones.

Countwheel: See Locking wheel.

Crutch: A fork-ended rod, being an extension of the escape-wheel arbor. The pendulum hangs through the fork or split in the crutch and is caused to swing by the impulse which the crutch gives it, having itself received the impulse from the escape wheel through the anchor. On regulators and semi-regulators the crutch often ends in a pin-like projection which slots into an elongated hole in the pendulum rod.

Fig. 17. The deadbeat escapement. The teeth of a deadbeat escape wheel are shaped very differently from those of an ordinary anchor escapement, of which the deadbeat is a modified form.

Dead-beat escapement: A refined form of anchor escapement, its invention usually credited to George Graham about 1715, though recent evidence suggests that the Fromanteels may have invented it. The escape-wheel teeth and the pallets of the anchor meet in such a way that there is not the recoil normally associated with an ordinary anchor escapement (which can be easily observed by watching the seconds hand of an anchor escapement clock as it takes one step forward and half a step back). The second hand stops dead at every tick. Figure 17 shows the principle. The dead-beat was used especially for precision clocks as it is superior for timekeeping, and is therefore normally found on regulators. It was less often used for domestic clocks as the more delicate wheel-teeth are prone to damage when the clock is being wound; it was very often combined with maintaining power (*q.v.*)

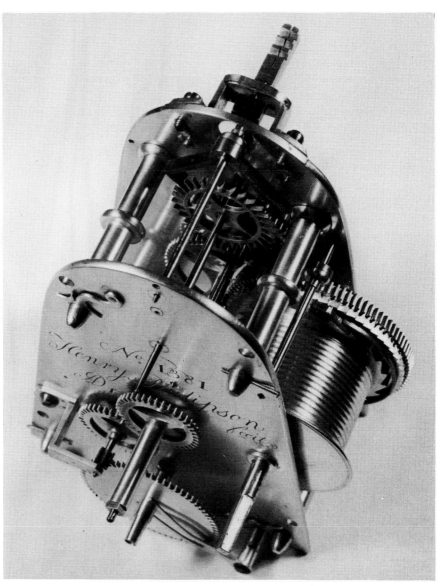

Plate 93. Regulator (with dial removed) made by Henry Philipson of Winster, Westmorland, and dated 1796. This maker here adopted the unusual practice of engraving his name, date and clock number onto the movement frontplate. He also, in this example, copied the unusual practice of his master, Jonas Barber junior, in fastening the plates by alternate latches and pins. The dead-beat escapement can be seen clearly. The three notches on the back-cock offer three options for the pendulum suspension spring to counter varying degrees of forward tilt in the case—a not unusual practice in better-quality longcase clockwork.

to avoid this potential tooth damage, and this escapement was also normally used on clocks built with a long centre-seconds hand, the reason being that such a long hand would otherwise have exaggerated the recoil action. Such a centre-seconds clock would not have maintaining power, as the seconds hand would then collide against the winding handle during winding; a centre-seconds clock should be stopped during winding.

Dial pillar: See Pillars.

Escape wheel: The wheel which connects with the anchor, or on pre-pendulum clocks it could refer to the crownwheel which connects with the verge. Sometimes called a 'scape wheel.

Falseplate: Sometimes called a backplate, but this term is not recommended because it is also used to refer to the movement backplate. An iron fixing plate used on japanned dials only, to help the clockmaker in attaching his movements. It was supplied by the dialmaker and was frequently impressed with his name, e.g. Wilson—Birmingham. Falseplates happened also to serve as convenient devices to assist when fitting a replacement movement to a brass dial, thereby giving us instant recognition of a 'wrong' brass-dial clock.

Finial: A decorative adornment often set on top of a clock hood as a pair, one to each side, or as a set of three according to the hood shape. Usually of brass but sometimes of gilded wood. Also used to describe the decorative top-piece of lantern-clock pillars. Brass finials are commonly of ball-and-spire or spreadeagle type. A torch and flame type is less common and usually in wood.

Fly: A rotating vane used to slow down what would otherwise be the rapid rate of striking of a clock. It is situated at the top of the strike train. A fly is also used to regulate the speed of a musical or chiming clock on the appropriate train.

Foliot: The European counterpart of the balance-wheel regulator and not used in Britain (except on turret clocks). It was a centrally pivoted rod with adjustable sliding weights at each end to slow it down or speed it up.

Gongs: A gong is usually a coiled spiral steel wire attached at one end and free to reverberate from the other when struck by a hammer. Gong striking is hardly ever found in British longcase clockwork until the late nineteenth century. It is common however to find strikework converted to a gong from a bell. This conversion can usually be recognised by the spare screw and steadypin holes left in the plate where the bellstand was previously attached. Conversion gongs were commonly attached to the case backboard on longcase clocks. Bracket clocks commonly have gongs from the early nineteenth century.

Grand Sonnerie striking: A system of chiming the hours and quarters so that one can tell the hour by the sound alone. The quarters are sounded in the normal quarter-chiming manner (i.e. by a ting-tang or by a chime of bells) and then the last hour is sounded too. Such a clock therefore has to have a very great store of power for this transmission and *grande sonnerie* striking is very unusual in British work. It is sometimes found in bracket clocks but in longcase work it is extremely rare.

Latches: Sometimes called latchets. On clocks this term refers to the method by which the pillars are held in place, usually movement pillars, less commonly dial pillars (in which latter case dial pillars are usually specified). A latch takes the form of a small catch, pivoted at one end by a rivet with its free end able to drop into a groove in the projecting pillar-end. Latches are usually shaped in a decorative manner. They are often a sign of higher quality work and therefore to some extent to be expected on much seventeenth-century London work. On provincial work they are unusual and their presence is then a more likely pointer to fine work. (See plate 93.)

The purpose of latches is to enable a workman to assemble or dismantle the plates more easily than with the taper-pin method. One sensible system sometimes found on provincial clocks is to have a latch on the centre pillar of a five-pillar movement, with taper pins on the four corner pillars. This system can sometimes be the sole justification for having a fifth pillar. Provincial clocks usually have only four pillars and hence do not have latches, though an occasional maker used latches on all four or just even two of the four at alternate corners.

It is difficult to imagine a slovenly workman taking the trouble to cut decorative latches, as these were hidden from the general view of his customer and would be of more help to later clock cleaners or restorers than to the maker himself.

Lenticle: Sometimes called a lenticle glass. An aperture in the door of a clock case, usually circular, sometimes octagonal, generally glazed with an air-bubble bottle-glass pane but sometimes a plain glass was used. Its purpose is believed to have been to allow the glint of the brass pendulum bob to be seen, though its function may have been to show the weight-lines as a reminder for winding.

Locking-wheel striking: Sometimes known as locking-plate or less commonly as countwheel or countplate striking. A notched wheel which controls the number of hours to be struck. It was the only system of striking prior to about 1676, after which rack striking (q.v.) gradually replaced it on many, but not all, longcase clocks. The clock is allowed to strike while a control arm, called a lifting-piece, is held out of the notch and prevented from striking while the arm rests in the notch. Hence the normal one-to-twelve succession of hours is achieved by having progressively wider spaces between notches. Complex variations can be used to include half-hour striking, Roman striking (q.v.) etc. Figure 18 shows the principle.

While rack striking quickly replaced this form on clocks of eight-day duration or longer, locking-wheel striking was retained on thirty-hour clocks, lantern and longcase, until they ceased production. On thirty-hour clocks this form of striking is normal at all periods and is *not* an indication of age. On some provincial eight-day clocks, especially those from certain regions such as Lancashire, locking-wheel striking was often retained until the 1770s.

The earliest position for locking wheels (on eight-day examples) was outside the backplate, called 'outside locking-plate action'. Thirty-hour clocks had outside locking-plate action throughout their entire history, except where a thirty-hour was made as a repeater, in which case, of course, it would have rack striking. By the later seventeenth century locking wheels on eight-day clocks became positioned inside the plates (known as 'inside locking-wheel striking') beside the striking-barrel wheel, known as the great-wheel and being the first wheel in the strike train. This change of position occurred about 1680 on London clocks, but later with some examples.

On some provincial thirty-hour clocks, particularly north-country examples, the outside countwheel is not of the normal notched type but may be a wheel carrying pins at ever-increasing distances and on these

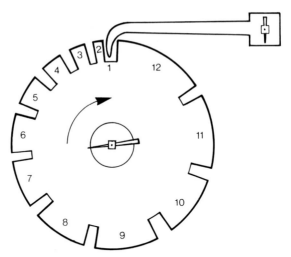

Fig. 18. Locking-wheel striking. The clock is allowed to strike when the control arm is held out of a slot and can slide on the wheel edge. Each space is graduated to give the normal numbered sequence, as shown in the diagram, the wheel itself does not normally bear numbers, except for one or two rare London clocks of the seventeenth century.

examples the control arm drops in the gap between pins during striking. This variation is quite commonly met with.

If a clock with locking-wheel striking gets out of sequence (as it might if the clock ran down) then it will stay out unless it is deliberately put into sequence again. This is done by lifting the control arm. Assuming the clock weight is in position, it will strike the next hour each time it is lifted until the right one is reached. This should not be done at 'warning' time, between about five minutes to and the hour, or it may not strike. On some thirty-hour clocks a small shaped finger-trip projects from the control arm arbor at the side of the clock for ease of re-setting without the need for groping blindly behind the movement.

Maintaining power: Very early eight-day clocks (e.g. plates 4 and 9) often had maintaining power, a device to keep the clock running while being wound, when otherwise the act of turning the key would remove the driving power (weight or spring) causing loss of the time taken to wind; possible damage to the teeth of the escape wheel, which on some clocks will rotate *backwards* when not being driven; and a negative time-count

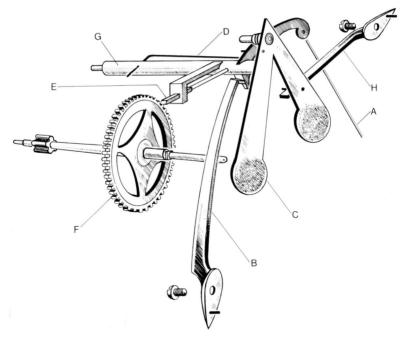

Fig. 19. Bolt and shutter maintaining power, taken from a clock by Henry Hindley of Wigan, 1725. The pullcord, *A*, tensions the bladespring, *B*, a pin on which pushes aside the shutters, *C*, which are pivoted on the back of the dialplate (not shown). The maintaining bolt spring, *D*, allows the bolt, *E*, to slide past the teeth of the centre wheel, *F*, as the bolt lifts ready to engage. Once the bolt is engaged the tension of the bladespring exerts a downward push on the bolt through the arbor, *G*, forcing the centre wheel to rotate clockwise. After disengagement the shutter return spring, *H*, pushes the shutters back into position.

shown by anti-clockwise rotation of escape wheel which would more than double the time loss shown by the clock hands.

The principle of maintaining power is that a blade spring keeps the action going during winding—in the case of a bracket clock is it a *second* spring. The earliest type was called bolt and shutter maintaining power. The winding key could not be inserted until the shutters which blocked the winding holes had been drawn aside by pulling a cord or sometimes a lever. This action simultaneously brought into play the 'bolt', a spring-pushed rod which pressed against the teeth of a going-train wheel, usually the centre wheel, i.e. the second one in the train, as this needed much less driving pressure than the great-wheel. This system was not so commonly used on spring-driven clocks, perhaps because their inaccuracy was such that this winding-time error would have been trivial.

Bolt and shutter power was very often removed in the past, presumably because the trivial advantages it gave were thought to be less of an asset than the potential problem which can arise whereby, if the bolt gets wedged tightly between wheel teeth, it can jam the whole clock train. This maintaining power system was sometimes used *without* the shutters. Where shutters are present there are two of them to cover both winding holes, though of course the striking-train shutter is purely to match up with the going one in appearance, there being no maintaining power on strikework.

A later type of maintaining power is named after John Harrison, who is credited with its invention in the early eighteenth century. It was used particularly for precision longcase clocks such as regulators, especially those having a dead-beat escapement with delicate teeth. It consists of a second ratchetwheel alongside the great-wheel. Power stored in a spring is released by the act of winding, thereby taking over the drive of the clock until winding is done. Bolt and shutter maintaining power fell out of use as the Harrison type came in, maintaining power thereafter being fitted only to precision clocks, especially regulators.

Thirty-hour clocks, driven by the figure-eight endless-rope system as devised by Huygens, already had their own permanent maintaining power, in so far as even during winding the pull of the weight is never removed from the going train. It *is* removed from the strike-train, but this does not matter.

Movement: Correct term for the 'works' of a clock or watch.

Pillars: The pillars are the corner posts, usually made of brass, which hold together the front and back plates of a plate-framed clock movement. They are usually rivetted into one plate, generally the back one, and held to the other by taper pins, which pass through holes in their extremities. Sometimes they fasten by means of latches, *q.v.*

Four pillars are adequate for all normal purposes and tend to be standard practice. Early London clocks quite often had five or even six pillars, supposedly for extra strength, though in many instances four would have sufficed. Because of the presence of more than four pillars on many early clocks, this gradually has come to be regarded as a sign of high-quality work. In practice, however, this can be misleading as London-area movements commonly have five pillars, even on stereotyped work of a mediocre nature of the later eighteenth or early nineteenth century. Quality cannot therefore be deduced from the number of pillars alone.

On provincial work and particularly in northern Britain the presence of five or more pillars would be exceptional and may very well be one indication of high-quality work. On the other hand many of even the most capable provincial makers never felt the need to use more than four pillars on straightforward movements.

Abnormal purposes might well dictate the need for more than four pillars on clocks from any area—as for instance with clocks of longer than eight-day run; musical clocks; clocks with automata or clocks carrying an unusually heavy load by virtue of special features (especially heavy weights).

Dial pillars, sometimes called dial feet, are used to join the dial to the movement frontplate.

Pillars usually exhibit decorative turnings and fins, which decorations can serve as an indication of age and/or quality; although it is a simplification, generally speaking the most decorative turnings indicate greatest age, though some makers on occasion deliberately produced finely shaped pillars which can appear very much out of period. For example, Samuel Deacon of Barton (Leicestershire) sometimes made fine baluster pillars in the later eighteenth century which resemble those of Edward East in the late seventeenth.

Pinion: A pinion has leaves, usually a small number such as six, and differs from a wheel (which has teeth) in that the 'wheel' part of a pinion is solid. A clock arbor usually carries a wheel at one end, through which it transmits power, and a pinion at the other end, through which it is driven by the next wheel in the train. The word pinion really refers to the leaved section only, but it is often more loosely applied to refer to the whole of a pinion plus its arbor. (See figure 15.)

On very early clocks the pinion leaves were filed by hand from solid steel rod. With the introduction of pinion wire in the later seventeenth century the clockmaker was able to buy this by the yard. Pinion wire was 'drawn' into shape by forcing it through drawplates of increasingly smaller bore until the required size of leaf was obtained. The clockmaker, having bought his ready-drawn pinion wire, simply made the arbor-with-pinion by turning off any leaves from all but the required leaf width, and the remaining central shaft became the arbor.

On early clocks the pinion width was only just sufficient to meet up with its particular wheel. However by Victorian times it was found preferable to leave an over-width span of pinion leaves so that as the leaves began to show signs of wear, the wheel to which the pinion connected could be moved along its arbor, thereby providing a new contact with the unworn section of pinion. A finished pinion was hardened and tempered before use. Although the steel pinion was harder than the brass wheel to which it engaged, pinions almost always show more wear than wheels. This is because grit embeds itself in the softer brass wheel-teeth and then abrades the steel pinion-leaves, leaving the brass comparatively unworn.

Pivot: The reduced end-section of an arbor, which butts into the bearing point of a clockplate. The pivot therefore carries the whole weight and strain of the power-source (weight or spring) and is very subject to wear. The section of the clockplate which houses a pivot is called a pivot-hole. With use pivots and pivot-holes can become badly worn, resulting in a sloppy fit. This is remedied by fitting a 'bush' in the brass plate, a bush being a circular brass washer-like piece fitting tightly into a plate to give a new bearing-surface.

Rack striking: Sometimes called rack repeating striking or rack-and-snail striking. A system of striking which superseded locking-plate striking and is usually credited as being the invention of Father Edward Barlow, a Catholic priest, about 1675–80. His name at birth was Booth and he took up the surname of Barlow later in life. It is by no means certain that it *was* Barlow's invention and his credit for it is based solely on the statement made by William Derham in his book *The Artificial Clockmaker* (1696) which statement all subsequent writers seem to have accepted without question. The date 1676 so often quoted for this invention is merely Derham's estimated date and is not a fact.

Barlow was born in 1639 at Warrington, Lancashire, was in Lisbon from 1659, returned to England in 1670 to work as a family priest in Yorkshire and then lived at Charnock Richard from 1672 until his death in 1719. It is known that he was in communication with Thomas Tompion and applied for a patent in 1686 for a *pull*-repeating device (not the same thing as rack-and-snail repeating). However his application was unsuccessful and his device was rejected in favour of one submitted by Daniel Quare, which received the approval of the Clockmakers' Company and of the clockmaking fraternity in general, several of whom were said *already* to be making similar repeaters. We appear to have no actual evidence that rack striking had

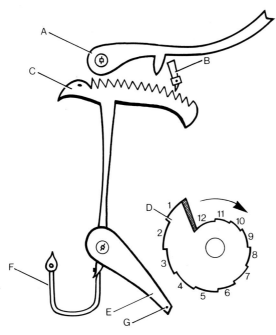

Fig. 20. Rack striking. The spring, *F*, pushes the rack, *C*, to the left to make available to the gathering pallet, *B*, the required number of teeth according to the hour. How far the rack moves to the left is determined by the rack pin, *G*, which contacts with the stepped edge of the snail, *D*. This system allows the same hour to be repeated as often as desired, and is therefore sometimes called the rack repeating system. Other labelled parts are: *A*, the rack hook; *E*, the rack tail.

anything to do with Edward Barlow, whose claim to fame on that account is no more than a legend.

In rack striking the number of blows struck was controlled by a 'snail', which was attached in such a way that it could not come out of sequence with the hour hand—this being the great failing of locking-wheel striking. This meant that a clock could be made to repeat the hour (or even the quarter hours) as many times as one wished, an exercise which was not quite so purposeless as might first appear. (See Repeating work.)

Figure 20 explains the principle. When the strikework is released the rack is pushed by a spring into the position where it will allow the correct number of blows to be struck. This position is determined by a stop-pin in the rack tail, which pin comes to rest against the chamfered spiral shoulder of the snail. This allows the rack proper to be pushed to the left until the appropriate number of teeth are exposed. These will then be counted along

245

by the rotating gathering-pallet. After striking the rack is held still by the rack hook.

Rack striking was much more quick to replace locking-plate striking on bracket clocks than on longcase clocks, where the old system was commonly used until the early eighteenth century on London work and considerably later in some provincial areas, especially in Lancashire.

On early clocks the rack and snail may be positioned between the movement plates, in which case it is called 'inside-rack striking'. Eventually it became established between the frontplate and the dial, where it is found on the great majority of eight-day clocks. Thirty-hour clocks always retained the locking-plate system, except in those unusual instances where repeating work was called for on a thirty-hour movement.

Regulator: A precision clock, usually of very high craftsmanship, made for accuracy rather than ornament and therefore generally at the expense of all other factors, often including beauty. Frequently of austere appearance, some Victorian examples are extremely ugly. They were often made for a clockmaker's own use in his timing of other clocks. Almost always non-striking, they frequently have precision escapements of a most ingenious nature, commonly including dead-beat escapements and often with maintaining power of one of the several varieties. Most are of longcase form but there are three-quarter-length wall versions. (Not to be confused with Vienna Regulators, mass-produced glass-fronted wall-clocks imported into Britain in large numbers in the later nineteenth century.)

Repeating work: A device whereby the last strike or chime of a clock, or both, may be repeated at will, usually by pulling a cord. It involves the use of rack strikework, *q.v.* It is often described as being a rare feature on longcase clocks, but this is certainly not so with provincial clocks, where repeating work is common on eight-day examples right through the eighteenth century and up to about 1820, after which it is uncommon. It sometimes occurs on thirty-hour clocks too. The presence of repeating work is usually a sign of quality, as a maker who was cutting corners would not as a rule have gone to this trouble, involving as it does a snail cut and positioned with much more precision than is needed with a non-repeater. A carefully cut and positioned snail will permit accurate repeating of the last hour at any time once that hour has struck until a few minutes prior to priming time (sometimes called warning time) for the next hour. This is achieved through the presence of a purpose-made long repeater spring attached to the front-plate and often rising vertically between pins on the lifting-piece, though some repeater springs lie horizontally and some start vertically and bend into a horizontal plane. A cord can usually be attached through a hole in the end of this repeater spring, the free end being allowed to hang down inside the case or sometimes to pass out of a hole in the hood or case side, on occasions by means of a small pulley-wheel for free running.

It is sometimes argued that a piece of string tied to the end of any lifting piece will enable the clock to be 'repeated'. This is true to a point, but if this is done it will be found that the clock repeats the last hour till about half-past, when it will change to striking the approaching hour. This is because such a clock was not designed as a repeater and the snail cutting is not accurate enough. The presence of the repeater spring indicates a true repeater. Its purpose is to ensure that the cord returns without snagging and thereby enables the lifting piece to drop back into its correct place after repeating. On some repeaters a starwheel is fitted to ensure precise repeating until priming time is reached. Starwheel repeaters are uncommon.

On a repeating clock the strike train often has gearing that contains extra power beyond that needed for ordinary striking. This means that if the repeating feature is *not* used, the strike train can be seen to be perhaps only two-thirds run down after eight days, while the going train has run down fully. This feature, together with the presence of a repeater spring (or the hole that once held its screw) enables one to recognise a repeating movement.

The purpose of longcase repeating work is not known; its use has been forgotten with many years of neglect of these clocks, but the fact that customers originally paid extra to have this feature made specially, indicates that it had a use which was then valued. It may have been used as a sort of alarm bell to call members of the family together, for instance at mealtimes, or perhaps to rouse the family from their beds to breakfast, but these are just suggestions.

Repeating work on bracket clocks is much more common, but is often of a different nature, usually called *pull-repeating*. With such a system the act of pulling the cord winds up a spring containing enough power for that one repeat performance, whether of hour repeating, quarter-hour repeating, or both. This pull-repeat system can therefore be found even on bracket clocks which have no striking train as the pull-repeat feature is a self-contained and self-powered unit.

On many bracket clocks the repeating work is driven from the striking spring, which then has to contain sufficient power to run the strike for eight days *and* allow for repeating at will. It was this problem, of power storage in a spring, which gave rise to self-winding pull-repeating. Repeating work on bracket clocks is said to have been of assistance in establishing the time in the dark, such as in an unlit bedroom, but this is not known for certain.

Roman striking: A method of striking which is economical in the use of driving power, being of particular benefit in spring clocks of long duration, especially in a month clock or a year clock. Its invention is ascribed to Joseph Knibb about 1680, apparently because his clocks are the earliest to employ this system. A few other makers used it later though it is such a rare feature that one is unlikely to come across it outside of the dozen or so well-known examples.

The principle is that two bells are used (but see also Ting-tang striking), a high-pitched bell which counts as one and a lower-pitched one which counts as five. The one and five bells are used in the same combinations as the Roman numerals on the dial—hence the origin of the name. One is therefore struck by a blow on the I bell, five is a blow on the V bell. Four o'clock is therefore I+V, seven is V+I+I, ten is V+V, eleven is V+V+I, and so on.

On most clock dials four is shown as IIII; on a clock with Roman striking it is shown as IV. However, the presence of IV on a dial does not necessarily mean that it has Roman striking.

Silvering: Generally speaking the engraved areas on brass-dial clocks were silvered originally. The chapter ring, seconds ring, calendar features, engraved centres and name-bosses are all features which commonly carried engraving on a plain background and therefore were silvered. Engraving on a *matted* background, as with some provincial dial-centres, could not be silvered.

Dials sometimes described as brass-and-steel or brass-and-pewter are usually in fact brass dials with silvering on some surfaces and are described incorrectly out of ignorance. Silvering was done by an application of silver chloride paste sealed by lacquering the surface. The lacquer eventually loses its quality and then the silver 'goes off'. Good restorers can re-silver a dial by the traditional process.

Ting-tang striking: A method of indicating the quarter-hours musically without the complexity of full chime work. It uses, in addition to the hour bell, a high-pitched bell (ting) and a low-pitched bell (tang). The clock strikes ting-tang once at quarter-past, twice at half-past, three times at quarter-to, and four times on the hour, followed by the hour count struck on a third bell. Normally a separate train of wheels is used to drive the ting-tang, and such a clock would therefore have three trains. Sometimes a ting-tang chime can be operated by the ordinary strike-train (which then must contain much more power-supply); such a clock would have only two trains. Ting-tang striking is rare on thirty-hour clocks.

Recommended Reading

Baillie, G. H. *Watch and Clock Makers of the World,* Volume I (1969) (see also under Loomes)

Beeson, C. F. C. *Clockmaking in Oxfordshire* (Antiquarian Horological Society 1967)

Bellchambers, J. K. *Devonshire Clockmakers* (Torquay 1962)

—*Somerset Clockmakers* (Antiquarian Horological Society 1969)

Brown, H. Miles. *Cornish Clocks and Clockmakers* (Newton Abbot 1970)

Bruton, Eric. *The Longcase Clock* (second edition, 1977)

Ceskinsky, H. & Webster, M. R. *English Domestic Clocks* (1913 re-published 1969)

Daniel, John. *Leicestershire Clockmakers* (Leicester 1975)

Edwardes, E. L. *The Grandfather Clock* (Altrincham 1971)

—*The Story of the Pendulum* (Altrincham 1977)

—*Weight-driven Chamber Clocks* (Altrincham 1965)

Goodison, Nicholas. *Gillows' Clock Cases* (Antiquarian Horological Society 1968)

Haggar, A. L. & Miller, L. F. *Suffolk Clocks and Clockmakers* (Antiquarian Horological Society 1974)

Lee, R. A. *The First Twelve Years of the Pendulum Clock* (Byfleet 1969)

—*The Knibb Family Clockmakers* (Byfleet 1964)

Legg, E. *Clock and Watch Makers of Buckinghamshire* (Fenny Stratford 1975)

Lloyd, H. Alan. *Old Clocks* (1958)

Loomes, Brian. *Country Clocks and their London Origins* (Newton Abbot 1976)

—*Lancashire Clocks and Clockmakers* (Newton Abbot 1975)

—*The White Dial Clock* (Newton Abbot 1974)

—*The Clockmakers of Great Britain* (in preparation)

—*Westmorland Clocks and Clockmakers* (Newton Abbot 1974)

—*Watch and Clock Makers of the World*, Volume II (1976) (see also under Baillie, G. H.)

—*Yorkshire Clockmakers* (Clapham 1972)

Mason, Bernard. *Clock and Watch Making in Colchester* (1969)

Moore, Nicholas. *Chester Clocks and Clockmakers* (Chester 1976)

Peate, Iorweth C. *Clock and Watch Makers in Wales* (Cardiff 1960)

Ponsford, Scott & Authers. *Clocks & Clockmakers of Tiverton* (Tiverton 1977)

Royer-Collard, F. B. *Skeleton Clocks* (1969)

Smith, John. *Old Scottish Clockmakers* (1921 re-published 1975)

Symonds, R. W. *A Book of English Clocks* (1947)

—*Thomas Tompion*; *His Life and Work* (1951 re-published 1969)
Tyler, E. J. *European Clocks* (1968)
—*The Craft of the Clockmaker* (1973)
Tebbutt, Laurence. *Stamford Clocks and Watches* (Stamford 1975)

Acknowledgements

Acknowledgements are due to the following people and organizations:—
Colin Andrew; David Barker; W. Clay-Dove; C. J. Glazebrook; Lewis
Hickson; E. Holmes; Ed LaFond; Bernard Mason OBE; C. Moore, Curator
of the Grosvenor Museum, Chester; Brian Morrison; Northamptonshire
County Council; Peter C. Nutt; F. Schomper; W. A. Seaby MA, FSA, FMA;
Strike One Ltd; Mr. and Mrs. P. F. Sykes; Charles Taylor; Archives Depart-
ment, Westminster City Libraries.

Especial thanks are due to the proprietors of The Dusty Miller Gallery,
Low Laithe, near Harrogate, North Yorkshire for providing the majority of
the illustrations of clocks which have passed through their hands.

Index

The subject sections are indicated at the head of each chapter and these are not repeated in the index. The lists of major makers in Chapter 12 are not repeated here. Page numbers in italics indicate figures and plates.